ALIAS EMPEROR RODGERS
A Majestic Memoir by Baltimore's Emperor of Insanity In The Crazy Daze of '60's Top 40 Radio

Paul H. D. Rothfuss

R | L Publishing, LLC
Winter Springs • Minneapolis

— — —

R | L Publishing, LLC
3524 Fourteenth Avenue South
Minneapolis, Minnesota 55407
WWW.RLPUBLISHERS.COM
612.840.2412

— — —

Because of the dynamic nature of the Internet, URLs or links contained in this book may have changed since publication. The author and publisher bear no responsibility for the persistence or accuracy of URLs for external or third party Internet websites referenced or linked in this publication, and does not guarantee that any content on such websites is, or will remain, accurate or appropriate.

Throughout this book you will find scannable QR codes in conjunction with hyperlinks. These have been provided for the reader's convenience. If the book is being read on a device that is not connected to the internet, a smartphone or tablet with a QR scanner can be used to immediately access the link and continue the reader's experience with the book. A free QR scanner is available at your favorite app store.

Original Cover Art by Erica Lehnhoff

ISBN: 978-1-7321623-1-0

CONTENTS

INTRODUCTION

We all have our favorite memories. The day we fell in love. The first glimpse of our new born children's faces. Our first job. The ladder we climbed in fulfilling our dreams. The people along the way who made it possible.

By extension, our memories are an extension of 'us'.

In the pages that follow, Paul Rothfuss has laid out his memories in writing like no other, all about those glorious (and not so glorious) days of the '50s and '60s when (thanks to Top Forty Radio) AM radio was supreme. Paul's recollections of getting started in broadcasting and where it led him enabled me to begin refreshing my own memories of those crazy days of Top Forty Radio, and the years before and after. Some of what I'd forgotten came rushing back to me. Yes, those days were crazy, but they were a lot of fun as well. To think we got paid for it. Memories.

There are a lot of similarities to our early years and how we each managed to develop careers in the business. We both married young and had children in our 20s, and we both started on a career path at about the same age. When we think back we marvel at how we did it. We wonder even more about some of the hijinks we experienced – Did we actually do that stuff? Great memories.

At one juncture, Paul 'became' Emperor Rodgers and, dressed in Julius Caesar-type attire, he rode elephants. All of us did 'record hops' and we met a lot of the stars of the Top 40 recording industry. We spent more time playing charity basketball – sometimes riding donkeys – than the hours we spent on the air. Then there were the loony on-air contests that you'll never again be able to pull off on radio.

The year the Beatles came to Baltimore, Paul chose to meet a client in Detroit. Paul got a brand new car out of the deal. I got to meet and interview the Beatles. Who got the better deal? Doesn't matter. Fond memories.

Top 40 Radio took us in different directions. Eventually, Paul realized his goal of owning a radio station…and not just one. In my case, there was an unexpected turn into television news. But throughout we have maintained a firm bond and friendship that has lasted fifty-five years. Wow! The memories.

Whether or not you grew up when Top Forty Radio was king, or you're simply curious about those days (daze?) and the men who made it possible, I'm sure you'll find Paul's story fascinating, informative and funny.

It might even stimulate your own memories like it has for me.

— Frank Luber
WCBM Radio
Baltimore, MD

PREFACE

So...a kid grows up in a small town in North Central Pennsylvania. One night at age fourteen (1954) he unwittingly tunes his AM radio to a distant station where he hears an iconic disc jockey 'talkin' jive' and spinnin' tunes the kid had never heard before – records by black artists whose 'rhythm and blues' styles were banned from nearly all of the 'white' radio stations of the day.

"If yer sittin' still with Fats an' "Blueberry Hill" you got a hole in yer soul. But if ya did you wouldn't be listenin' to ol' John R., 'cause I got me some soul, too."

The kid falls in love with the patter and the music.

He knows nothing about being on the radio, but on a whim he shows up at a local radio station seeking an audition. At age seventeen he's hired @ 0.85c per hour. By twenty-three he's doin' mornings on the legendary WCAO, the runaway number-one-rated radio station in Baltimore, Maryland.

Who knew the kid would work with a DJ who'd set the news copy on fire while the kid was reading it. Or that he'd say 'no' to an opportunity to introduce the Beatles in exchange for getting a new car for a year. Or that he'd be crowned 'Emperor' and be strolling downtown Baltimore streets with a mountain lion on a gold chain, or riding donkeys up and down a basketball court, or an elephant down Maryland Avenue.

Emperor Rodgers

Such were the crazy daze of 1960's Top Forty Radio. Stuff like this was happening (going on) at Top Forty Radio Stations all over America.

The kid stayed on the air for seventeen years, moved to media sales and management for two more, and with Kerby Scott followed it all up with three decades as the 'wild and crazy' owner and operator of over fifty radio stations. (A story for another book.)

To quote Bob Parsons, founder of GoDaddy.com: When you love something it will give you all of its secrets.

I'm that kid. I fell in love with radio broadcasting and radio responded generously with its secrets. I loved radio. As a result I've never had to "work" for a living.

However, I am still waiting for some monogrammed shirts.

Our story unfolds here. We hope you'll enjoy it.

—Paul H. D. Rothfuss

CHAPTER ONE

B2B

History records little of import occurring on September thirteenth.

September 13, 122 saw the beginning of construction on Hadrian's Wall.

On September 13, 1224, St. Francis of Assisi was afflicted with stigmata, and in 1579 Breda formed the Union of Utrecht. Not great news for Francis. Nice if you were a northern Utrechtian.

On Sept. 13, 1789, New York City banks made their first loans to the US Government. You know what they say. "Lie down with dogs..."

September 13, 1942 was a really bad day for Chicago Cub shortstop Leonard Merullo. He made four errors in one inning. Yet, Eastern Flevolanders saw Sept. 13, 1956 as a very good day, the day the dike surrounding them was closed.

TV viewers and Rock fans would probably assign importance to the events of Sept 13, 1961, 1973, and 2012, respectively.

In 1961 'Car 54 Where Are You' made its TV debut, and in 1973 Congress passed a bill lifting pro football's TV blackout policy.

Best of all, on 9/13/2012 Russian Prime Minister Dmitry Medvedev called for the Russian Punk Band 'Pussy Riot' to be freed from prison. Shortly thereafter a poll showed Russian men favoring Medvedev's decision by a factor of 81%, believing that any advocate for a free 'Pussy Riot' just had to be an OK guy.

In sports, Steve O'Shaughnessy scored 100 in thirty-five minutes in Lancs vs Leics, Sept. 13, 1983, tying the old record. No, really. Honest. He actually did.

Perhaps the most revered event ever to occur on September 13 was in 1503 when Michelangelo began working on his sculpture of David.

The result was impressive no matter how it's viewed. But I digress.

Sept. 13, 1940 saw Italian troops, under the command of Marshall Graziani, attack Egypt. 'Twas ol' Graz's finest hour.

And coincidentally, on that very same day in Williamsport, PA – 'Billtown' to the locals – I was born.

It was a Friday.

First Born

I am my parents' first child. Paul A. Rothfuss, MD, my Dad, was a Family Doctor and General Surgeon. Born at home in 1893, the fourth of nine children, he grew up on the family farm in Upper Fairfield Township - 'Out in the sticks' he used to say.

At fifteen Dad graduated from eighth grade at the one-room school- house, attended Muncy Normal School, and at seventeen returned as the teacher at that very same schoolhouse. Later he graduated from Susquehanna College (now University), and in 1923 from the University of Maryland Medical School.

Paul Arndt Rothfuss, M.D.

Nettie Maria Louisa Duncombe, my Mom, was the daughter of Tyrrell H. A. Duncombe, a pharmacist and inventor, and Nettie Maria Merritt, both of St. Thomas, Ontario, Canada where my mother was born on May 29, 1908.

Mom was a beautiful girl with black hair and sparkling dark eyes. She was a trained concert pianist with a 'slap-sticky' sense of humor. Mom was a wonderful friend to all and a benefactor to many…a true caregiver.

Nettie Maria Louisa Duncombe

In a strange course of events, my parents met in 1925 at the Hialeah Race Track in Miami, Florida. Dad was employed as the Physician On Duty, to serve in case any of the patrons fell ill. Mom was on a date with one of her Flapper boyfriends.

Dad was 32, Mom was 17.

They married five years later.

Mine were outstanding parents.

––––––––

I can't remember much about World War II but I do remember starting school in September, 1946 at the J. Henry Cochran Elementary School. I entered school in the second grade.

I think I was a happy kid.

Kilocycles

Fast-forward to 1952, 12 years old, when my mom gave me a Philco table model radio. Dark purple, AM only, two knobs: On/Off-Volume and Tune.

5% taller and a bit wider than a loaf of bread.

1950 Philco Model 50-520 "Transitone" Tube Radio in Bakelite Case

A medium sized, triangular shaped wedge had broken away from the top cover, so when I listened at night the tubes glowed against my bedroom wall.

At age twelve I loved baseball on the radio. (Still do.) Dialing around one night I stumbled onto a Cardinals/Phillies game. A voice said, "You're listening to Cardinals baseball on KMOX in St. Louis, Missouri."

What? It's a long haul from St. Louis to Williamsport. I had no idea how this was possible. I was astounded.

Next morning I greeted my Dad with, "Hey Dad. Last night I heard a radio station from St. Louis!"

"St. Louis, huh? We'll have to look into it."

Dad seemed unimpressed. I wanted more.

That night I went at it in earnest, dialing around and finding stations from far, far away. WCKY Cincinnati, WWVA Wheeling, WCBS New York, WLW New Orleans, WBZ Boston and stations from Toronto, Chicago, Detroit, Nashville.

Many still carried network programs – TV with no pictures except those seen in the theatre of the mind. A few carried baseball games. One or two played music.

Note: Later I learned that I'd been 'DXing,' defined as 'the hobby of dialing around a radio band hoping to find distant radio stations'. ('DX' is telegraphic shorthand for 'distant'.)

AM radio signals can cover huge distances at night. When the sky wave is 'right' the high-powered AM stations that are alone at their spot on the dial (called 'clear channel' stations) can cover unbelievable distances.

Radio Morphs

By 1954 TV had stolen most of the 'programs' from radio, and music was just beginning to become the staple for radio programming. Coincidentally, Rock 'n' Roll was starting to push aside the pop music of the day.

'The Lucky Strike Hit Parade' was one of the top-rated shows on TV. Each week Dorothy Collins, Russell Arms, Giselle McKenzie and Snooky Lanson (yes, he was called Snooky) would sing/perform the seven songs that topped the music charts that week.

This worked great when the hits were "Teach Me Tonight" or "Oh My PaPa" or "Doggie In The Window," but when rock 'n' roll music started making its way to the top of the charts the aforementioned stars proved incapable of providing renditions that were acceptable to the now-younger audience watching the show.

Rock 'n' roll smashed into "Your Hit Parade" like a Sugar Ray Robinson right-cross. Show producers tried to fight back by presenting the songs in humorous skits, but soon discovered that the audience was mostly laughing at the singers rather than with them.

I mean really. Crooner Snooky Lanson doing "Hound Dog?" Giselle McKenzie singing "Jim Dandy?" Russell Arms taking a crack at "Great Balls Of Fire?"

These desperate attempts to save the show proved futile. By 1958 'Your Hit Parade' was off the air, drowned in the tidal wave of hits by Fats Domino, Buddy Holly, LaVerne Baker, The Dubs, Little Richard, Gene Vincent and the Blue Caps, Dinah Washington, and of course, the immortal Elvis Presley.

Hail, Hail

The long-distance stations playing music were a godsend to anyone in Williamsport under the age of seventeen. No Billtown stations would have dared to play that music!

One fall night in 1954 the sky wave was delivering the goods 'clear as a bell'. I DXed my way to 1510 AM, WLAC out of Nashville, Tennessee. As the station boomed into Billtown, unknowingly, I was about to be fitted with my first pair of rock 'n' roll shoes.

"You're listening to John R. on WLAC in Nashville, Tennessee, brought to you by Ernie's Record Mart, 179 Third Avenue in Nashville, Tennessee. Tonight Ernie's Record Mart features the Big Blues Special ... six hit records for two ninety-eight plus shipping and handling, a total of just three dollars and ninety-nine cents.

"You get Johnny Ace (eight bars of 'Pledging My Love'), the Spaniels (eight bars of 'Goodnight Sweetheart, Goodnight'), Fats Domino (eight bars of 'Thinking of You'), and one from that sensational new cat, Elvis Presley (eight bars of 'That's All Right, Mama'). These records are honeys ... a gas ... hittin' an' gittin'. Send your check for three dollars and ninety-nine cents to Ernie's Record Mart Big Blues Special, 179 Third Avenue, Nashville, Tennessee. That's Ernie's Record Mart Big Blues Special, 179 Third Avenue, Nashville, Ten Ness See.

"Ernie's Record Mart, Nashville, Tennessee and ONLY Nashville, Tennessee, nowhere else in the WORLD! They got them records galore at that store.

"All right! For you Cool Cats and Charmin' Chicks ... here's the Five Keys with 'The Glory of Love.'"

At fourteen I'd never heard anything like John R. – the first honest-to-God for-realsie black "Disc Jockey" I'd ever heard. He was so damn coool. He gave new meaning to the word 'hip;' he was the 'hippest' of his day. He built his patter on phrases and accents of the African-American community, from which I knew he came. If this had been the sixties we'da said, "John R. is 'Outta' Sight."

Some of his early sponsors were 'White Rose Petroleum Jelly' and 'Silky Straight,' a hair-straightener favored by African Americans. I can still sing their jingles.

And of course, Ernie's Record Mart.

"Now, friends, I know you got some soul. If you din't you wouldn't be listenin' to ol' John R., 'cause I got me some soul, too. I'll tell you somethin' friends. You can really tell the world you got soul with this brand new Swinging Soul Medallion, a jewelry pendant that you're gonna love love love!"
[Insert ordering info here.]

John R. (Richbourg) was a selling machine.

WLAC was where I discovered the treasure trove of Doo Wop songs and real Rhythm and Blues music that I grew to love – especially Doo Wop.

Surprise, Surprise

I stopped listening to John R. in the early sixties but I couldn't forget this cool cat on the radio … the first black DJ I'd ever heard.

In March of 1974, well into my radio career, there appeared on my desk a picture of John R. – the first picture of him I'd ever seen.

He was a white guy!

John "John R." Richbourg

Mr. R, you had me fooled for thirty years.

I can still hear him in my mind's ear:

"Hunka down an' grab-a holt ta this one from Little Richard."

And Richard said, "Long Tall Sally she's … built sweet. She got … evr'thang that Uncle John need … ohh baby."

John R. was just so damned cool.

Phases

My intro to rock 'n' roll came at age fifteen, as I was passing thru my James Dean phase. You know … pouty, slouchy, sullen? All for absolutely no reason.

This would be followed by my Elvis phase. Dark hair with a pompadour. Hair combed back on the sides into a DA. Black pegged pants and pink shirts.

Both of these phases were short-lived. Mom and Dad made sure of that.

Eventually I landed on my true self.

Remember 'Happy Days'? I was 65% Ritchie Cunningham and 35% Ralph Malph.

The Five Sharps

John R. introduced me to Doo-Wop music. The Five Key's "Ling Ting Tong," The Turban's "When You Dance," The Oriole's "Crying In The Chapel."

And of course, The Chord's "Sh-Boom." "Hey launy ding dong, sha-lang a lang a langa. Hahoom bow dip, ah doom ba doe ba dip – Ahh, life could be a dream … ."

The Chords

We never heard this version in Williamsport. Our stations played the 'cover' version by The Crew Cuts, four nice white boys from Canada.

The Crew Cuts

It was very nice and a smash hit, but it totally lacked the 'soul' and 'feel' of the original. No surprise. The original was recorded by the fellas that wrote the song.

I memorized these songs, especially the 'runs' sung by the bass man.

From Sh-Boom: "Every time I think of you, something is on my mind. If you do what I want you to, Baby, we'll be so fine."

I loved hearing these songs … and singing them.

Sooo … with my pal, Jack McCallus, we formed a Doo Wop Group with three of our high-school buddies. We were 'The Five Sharps' – Pat Abrunzo, Dave Luppert, Jack McCallus, Hess Wertz and me. Jack sang lead. I sang bass and played guitar. Pat, Dave and Hess sang some lead and added tenor and baritone parts. Wayne Kibbe accompanied us on the piano.

We covered hit songs of the day … songs like The Penguin's "Earth Angel" and of course, "Sh-Boom" … the Crew Cuts version.

We didn't know if we were good or bad, but the kids seemed to like us. We appeared in local talent shows and occasionally with the Johnny Nicholosi Orchestra.

We were having a ball.

Hey, every now and then we even got paid, like, twenty-five bucks.

It was never about the money. It was always about the fame, right?

Riiight!

How Do You Make A Hit Record?
In 1955, Channel 28 in Wilkes-Barre, PA announced a talent contest on Johnny Sobel's Bandstand program. We entered.

First prize was a Mercury Records recording contract ... or so we were told. Voting was via penny post cards sent by viewers.

Over a five-week period we appeared on TV four or five times, reaching the finals with two other contestants.

We topped the voting week after week and truly believed we'd win and be on our way to ...

But wait!

We finished second.

The first prize was won by (you won't believe it) ... a tap dancer!

Yep. A tap dancer won a Mercury Records recording contract.

Huh?

I can hear it now: "Oh Ba-Bee it's John R. spinnin' the hottest new recording by Little Timmy Mikashlevsky."

Tappity-tap-tap-tap-tippity-tapperoo.

Get that one tonight at Ernie's Record Mart."

Second prize was a five-piece collection of small electrical kitchen appliances – a blender, a toaster, a waffle iron, a hot plate and an electric knife.

How convenient. One appliance for each of us.

But hey! What teenage Doo Wop singer doesn't want a waffle iron?

We were that close!

Our final appearance was at our Senior Prom where we performed our cover version of the Del-Viking's 'Come Go With Me' and The Diamond's 'Little Darlin'.

And the bass man said, "My Darlin' … I need you … to call my own … and never do wrong. To hold in mine … your little hand. I'll know … too soon … that all is sooo grand. Pleeease … hold my hand."

God how I love Doo Wop music!

Top 40
Top 40 Radio arrived in 1955, having been birthed by the antics of Peter Tripp, Alan Freed and other 'hot jocks' of the day.

Williamsport radio featured NBC, CBS and Mutual.

Snooze radio. Zzzchzz.

No local station would have been caught dead playing that rock 'n' roll trash or that 'race music,' defined in that era as "any songs recorded by black people who were not big band singers." Louis Armstrong, yes. Fats Domino, no. (Later, this term was ditched and replaced by 'rhythm and blues'.)

Thanks to John R. I had fallen in love with the rock 'n' roll music of Elvis, Carl Perkins and Gene Vincent; with great Doo-Wop songs by the likes of The Dells, The Five Keys, and Lee Andrews and The Hearts; and with the great rhythm and blues sounds of Ivory Joe Hunter, LaVern Baker, Chuck Willis, Bill Doggett, etc.

And though I didn't recognize it at the time, I had fallen in love with radio.

Barbie, Before There Was 'Barbie'
1956 would be huge for me. I was to meet the girl I would marry. I'll introduce her later.

G-burg
High school graduation was June of 1957. Summer flew by, and on September 13 (my 17th birthday) I enrolled as a freshman at Gettysburg College.

I was an unsuccessful college student, capable but disinterested. Yet my year at G-burg would provide me with a very meaningful education, via osmosis.

Soon after arriving at college, and still a dedicated DXer, I found a Top 40 station out of Baltimore. WCAO – Baltimore's #1 rated station. A legend and a pioneer in the Top 40 format.

Bob Coolidge, Les Alexander, and Alan Drake were great Top 40 Radio Personalities. WCAO played 'our' music. They had great contests and did lots of whacky stuff.

They were sensational. I couldn't stop listening.

My grades reflected my disinterest in the rigors of college, but I was receiving a serious and totally free education in a different 'classroom,' in a 'major' that would shortly be revealed as my ideal fit. I had no idea.

Unintended consequences are sometimes positive.

CHAPTER TWO

EVER SINCE

At age fifteen my life was lived in 'dilemma world.' Irresponsibility clashed with duty several times daily, every decision fraught with the inevitability of review by the Supreme Court of Parental Justice.

Dad.

Wednesday evening was 'Library Night.' "Hey Dad. I'm going to the library to study."

Translation? "I'm going to watch Bob's basketball game. I'll be home around 9:30."

One Wednesday in mid-February, 1956, I found myself sitting about halfway up in the stands of the old gym. We're lounging, Bob Hakes and I, watching the jayvee game. It's halftime.

We are both so very cool - fannies hanging off of one bleacher seat, elbows on the seat behind us. Two high school juniors enjoying "Boys Night Out."

Note: Bob was a great looking guy, a 'girl magnet' who (it was alleged) knew every girl in town.

And there she was. Walking into the gym with her Curtin Jr. High School cheerleader pals, carrying a halftime Coke.

Adorable.

Tall. Dark hair. Great smile.

"Bob, who's that?"

"Who?"

"That dark haired girl with the cute smile ... the cheerleader ... the tall one."

"Ahmm, I dunno."

(Ohh, great. Really helpful.) "Thanks a lot."

Thursday, And The Search Is On

"Sure I know her. That's Barbie Love. She lives on Woodmont Avenue."

Words of value from by best pal, Don Smith.

"Yeah. I play softball with her brother. I'll introduce you in the Spring."

(Spring? Spring? I could be dead by then. That's not until May ... three more months? Are you nuts?)

"Love? Her last name is Love? Wow."

Mid-April

"Hey, why not stay at my house tonight?" It was Don. "We'll go to the dance and come here after. Bring your fishin' stuff so we're ready in the morning."

Mom gave me the OK and I packed my gear. We planned to leave early Saturday so we didn't stay long at the Friday night dance. No girls there. Not her anyway.

Back at Don's by ten. "Remember Don, you promised an introdution."

"You're still thinking about her? Hey. Why not call her right now and ask her to the Prom?"

"Geez, Don, I don't even know her."

"Butcha' want to, right? You're just chicken. I'm calling her."

Don was dialing.

"Aww, geez ... OK, OK. Gimme the phone."

I don't mind a challenge, but this one included trying to talk with an apple stuck in my throat.

Riiinnnggg !

(Raspy 'Dad voice') ... "HEL-oo."

"Mmay I please speak to m-buh m-Barbie?"

"BARBIE. PHONE." (phone drops – clunk!). Then in the background the Dad voice – "I don't know. It's a boy."

Her

"Hello."

"Barbie?"

"Yes."

I introduced myself, told her where I'd seen her, and then, as if I'd done this a dozen times before, up and asked this adorable ninth-grader that I'd never met if she'd be my date to the Williamsport High School Junior Prom.

"I can't go to any prom with you ... I don't even know you."

(Geez. Of course you do!)

"You know me. We were on the stage together in March, at the Curtin talent show. You tap-danced with your sister and I'm the bass singer with The Five Sharps."

"I don't remember."

"OK – but why does that matter?"

"It matters to my parents. Besides, I'm going steady."

(Can you say 'futility?')

None of this was what I'd hoped to hear and I have no recollection of the 'good-bye' part of the conversation.

I got another date for the prom.

If At First
It's May and time for 'the meeting'. A front yard softball game and a chance to impress.

Don's driving his MG and we pull in front of her house. Mr. Cool and Mr. Cool, Jr.

We say our hellos and start tossing the ball around with her brother, Jim.

Barbie's there.

Unimpressed doesn't come close to describing her reaction.

Chilly?

Try 'North Pole'.

But hey. It's early. I'm cool. I'm a rising senior.

Besides, I'm in love.

I 'brave up'. I disregard her nonchalance and vow to press on.

June
"Really Coach, the All Star team?"

Amazing. I'd played baseball since age twelve but was a poor hitter. Obviously, I'd never made an All Star team.

In my last year of Babe Ruth League they made me a relief pitcher. I had excellent control of a sorta slow 'fastball' and an array of slower stuff that included a baffling knuckleball.

A junk-baller at fifteen.

The strategy was for me to relieve our fastball pitchers. It worked like a charm.

First time through a lineup batters broke their backs trying to time my snail-paced pitches. I rode it all the way to the All Star team.

"First game's July 7. Practice starts June 28th."

I'd made it!

Eagles Mere

"Hey, wanna come up for the Fourth?"

Don had a summer job managing the 'Casino,' a teenage entertainment center that was part of the Forest Inn, a beautiful resort hotel in Eagles Mere, in the heart of Pennsylvania's Endless Mountains. Bowling, ping pong, pool, a jukebox for dancing and a neat snack bar.

"She's here. Bet you'll have better luck this time. Fourth's Wednesday. Come up Sunday."

Gulp!

————

My summers were spent working on our farm, baling hay and straw, detasseling corn, milking cows and taking care of horses. 'Busy' doesn't describe it.

July was hay and corn season. Milking was forever. Dad needed me there.

But I had to ask.

"Son, y'know there's hay to be made. But I guess it's OK. You can go Monday after work, but be home and ready for work Thursday morning. Don't forget, you have baseball practice."

"Thank you, Dad. Thank you. Thank youuuu!"

————

Monday evening at the Casino ... lots of people I didn't know and lots of music I liked. Nat "King" Cole's "A Blossom Fell," The Five Keys' "Out of Sight, Out of Mind," Elvis' "Blue Suede Shoes."

Don's working and I'm meeting people, making new friends.

And Barbie is here.

I'm totally smitten. Couldn't hide it. Wasn't tryin'.

Tuesday: Swimming at the lake ... a mob scene. Families mostly, and a bunch of teenagers. A beautiful lake surrounded by big trees and covered with sailboats, rowboats and canoes. A picture postcard. People having fun.

Swimming ... Frisbee ... sophomoric hijinks. It's summer.

I'm immortal and everything's right with the world.

––––––––

There were four large resort hotels in Eagles Mere. Each hotel had its own boathouse and dock on the lake, filled with canoes and rowboats for rental by the guests.

"They need a boat boy to run the Crestmont boat dock," says Don. "They asked me if I knew anybody. You interested?"

Life's scales are delicate and easy to tip.

On the one hand, an obligation to Dad and a spot on the All Star team.

On the other hand, Barbie.

Desire vs. duty = dilemma.

Heck, this one's easy!

"Ahhh, Dad? One of the hotels offered me a job today. A boat boy. Pay? Ahh, two bucks a day but I get room and board. May I accept? Yeah, I know about the hay, but it's almost all made, so … please? Great, Dad! Thanks! I'll be home tomorrow to get my stuff, but then I have to come right back so I can start work the next day. Thanks Dad!"

Note: I believe Dad gave his permission because he thought it a good idea for me to be away from home and sort of 'on my own' for a while. While he needed me at the farm, I think he saw this as a 'good experience' for me. Turns out he was 'righter' than he could've known.

———

"Coach, I can't be on the All Star team. I need to work the rest of the summer and my job starts in three days."

Situational ethics are always messy.

Workin' Man
July 6, 1956. First day on the job. There's nothing like a glorious, sunny morning alongside a pretty mountain lake. Good day to pursue the girl of my dreams, right? Makes sense to me!

But how?

Her brother, Jim, is the boat boy at the boathouse just across the lake. I see lots of activity over there. Looks like mostly girls. Bet she's there.

They're swimming off Jim's dock … having a wonderful time. Guess I'll sweep my dock. Maybe they'll notice.

A couple hours pass and there's nothing happening. Then – footsteps and giggling behind the boathouse. Hmmmm.

It was Barbie and some of her girlfriends.

"We came to see you 'cause it's your first day."

Just the encouragement I needed.

A Dance or Two

Lots of young people gathered at the Casino most every evening, but the crowds were bigger on the weekends. Many were folks who worked at the resorts. Many others, Barbie included, were cottagers who spent summer vacations in Eagles Mere.

That Friday evening Barbie and I had a Coke and a dance or two. Then some conversation … and my big moment.

"May I walk you home?"

The twenty-minute walk around the lake was pure magic. Up the hill we walked to her cottage, and a soft "g'night" at the patio door.

July 9

More footsteps. More giggling. This time it was a couple of her girlfriends, but no Barbie.

"Thought you should know – tomorrow's Barbie's birthday. See you at the Casino tonight."

I saw Barbie that evening at the Casino.

"Tomorrow's my birthday. Wanna come for dinner?"

I was absolutely floored.

"Yes. Thank you."

"See you around six?"

"OK."

July 10

Boats 'r' all up. Gotta' hurry. I'm goin' to a Birthday Party!

I walked around the lake and up the hill past an old gray cottage, where I saw pink climbing roses on a fieldstone wall.

A fine birthday guest I am. Got no money. Got no present.

Voila! The gift!

With my pocketknife I cut a couple of clusters of the pink roses.

Barbie was on the patio when I arrived.

"Happy Birthday, Barbie. I brought these for you."

"Roses. My favorite. Thank you."

(She has such a beautiful smile.)

The Love Family

I met Barbie's parents and her family. Dad, Mom, Granddad, brother and three sisters. Incredible people. Welcoming. Intelligent. Warm. Down to earth. And more fun than I can describe.

The delicious dinner was accompanied by birthday presents and much laughter. I was completely at ease.

I gave Barbie a teeny tiny kiss as I was leaving.

"I'll come see you tomorrow at the boathouse."

(Can't wait.)

I remember walking down the stone steps of the patio on the way back to my room and saying to myself, "I want to be like them."

July 10, 1956. To date this was the best day of my life!

July Into August

Sunny days at the dock ... Sweet summer nights at the Casino ... Walks around the Lake ... Goodnight kisses at the door.

(I'm very much in love. She's more than I dreamed of or could ever have hoped for.)

This is exhilarating. Is it possible to be free and be in prison at the same time?

August 11

Casino Saturday nights were always great. Big crowds of young peo- ple, lots of fun and lots of great music.

I could never have predicted that this particular Saturday night would be a defining moment of my life.

Barbie and I were dancing to The Platters' "(You've Got) The Magic Touch."

"Will you go steady with me?"

"Yes."

I looked at my watch. Saturday, August 11, 1956. Eight minutes past eleven.

I was going steady with Barbie Love...and she with me.

And ever since.

Barbara Allen Love, 1958

Post Script

On the day she was born, Barbie's parents called her their "Rosebud." Turns out, I was the first boy to give her flowers.

Years later Barbie told me that the 'gift' of those few stolen roses really got her attention – a tiny gesture that eventually led to our marriage and to the wonderful life we've shared.

Many years later it dawned on me: my Barbie was Barbie … before there was 'Barbie'.

Rosebud and Barbie. Suits her perfectly.

Can you believe it?

I married a girl named Barbie Love.

CHAPTER THREE

BEGINNING

Nine months without a car did not serve to enhance my collegiate performance.

Mobility is king. Wheels = mobility.

For me? No wheels and no-mo for ten whole months.

My wheels? A '53 Merc. Salmon color with white top and black fender skirts.

Freshman year was over. I'd been home for one whole day.

No eight o'clock classes, no finals, saw Barbie.

Everything's good.

Billtown Radio

So I'm cruisin' down Third Street around five-thirty on the afternoon of June 4th, 1958. A buddy had told me about a 'new' radio station on the air and it was playing "our music."

("Impossible. Williamsport [ergo: Billtown] stations never play 'our' music. We got NBC, CBS and Mutual. But 'our' music? Never. He musta been listening to some long distance station last night.")

"Yeah. They're in the South Williamsport Borough Building. On the second floor, above the police station."

As I passed the Central Music Store and the Keystone Theater I turned on my radio. I assumed I was wasting my time. Then again I had nothing to lose.

(Besides, when you're seventeen and crusin' you must have the radio on.)

I started low on the dial and worked my way up.

BAM! - I hit AM 1450, and out of the speakers came Chuck Berry and "Johnny B. Goode."

Stunned, I looked to see if it was NBC (WRAK), CBS (WWPA), or Mutual (WLYC).

Neither. This was a new station and 1450 AM was a 'new' frequency. I couldn't believe it.

It gets better.

A voice said, "That was Chuck Berry and 'Johnny B. Goode' on WMPT with Kerby Confer."

("That's Kerby Confer. Right there? On the radio? Wow!)

En Route

Right turn off Third Street onto Market, then across the Market Street Bridge to a right on Southern Avenue. I was making a beeline to the radio station.

Note: Kerby and I met in 1952 when we appeared together in a Christmas show at Thaddeus Stevens Junior High School. I was eighth grade, he was seventh. We weren't 'hang out' buddies but we knew and liked each other. I hadn't seen Kerby since before my graduation from Williamsport High School in May of '57.

Birth

I went up a very long staircase and stepped into the rectangular space that was the studio and offices of WMPT, "The Nifty Fourteen Fifty." The station facility shared half the upstairs space, walled off from an area where the Borough stored the costumes and other stuff for the annual Mummers Parade.

The rather spartan arrangement of six-hundred square feet was divided into three areas: Two 15 x 15 foot spaces, one an office and the other a meeting area – on either side of a 5 x 10 foot 'studio' with double glass windows on either side.

And there in that studio was my friend, Kerby Confer, surrounded by hundreds of 45's and albums.

"Paul! Great to see you. What's up?"

"I just got back from college and heard you on the radio. How in the world did you get started with this?"

Turned out that while stationed at Ft. Gordon in Augusta, Georgia, station owner Galen D. "Dave" Castlebury had applied for a new AM radio station license. (More on this later.) The FCC grant of the license application came just as Dave was mustering out of the Army. He immediately returned to Williamsport to build the facility.

––––––––

Kerby and one of his classmates, Fred Plankenhorn (also a friend) somehow got together with Dave and volunteered to help build the station.

While seniors in high school, Kerby and Fred became WMPT's first announcers. They were paid the handsome sum of $0.85 per hour, the minimum wage at that time.

Note: At this very same time I was attending Gettysburg College and listening to Baltimore's #1 Rated Station – WCAO, a pioneer in the new format that would be the savior of the radio industry: Top Forty. (Major connection to follow!)

Bug Bit
Kerb asked me to be quiet as he opened the mike and introduced another record. I watched. I was intrigued. Perhaps even a bit jealous.

"This looks like fun."

"It is, and we need an announcer. Why don't you come over tomorrow morning and audition?"

(I was always in plays and shows in school and I loved 'our' music. I'd never given a minute's thought to being on the radio.)

"Mmm, OK. Do I need an appointment?"

"Nah. Come over around ten. Mr. Castlebury's usually back from the transmitter by then. Tell him I told you to come in."

I couldn't sleep.

Words of Wisdom
"Ahh Yip yip yip yip yip yip yip yip
Mum mum mum mum mum mum
Get a job, sha na na na, sha na na na na."
— The Silhouettes. January, 1958

Aww Dishion
Wednesday, June 4, 1958 at ten AM, I climbed the steps to the radio station. I could never have imagined – or even thought about where these steps could someday lead.

"May I please speak with Mr. Castlebury?"

"I'm Dave Castlebury. Can I help you?"

"My name is Paul Rothfuss. Kerby Confer told me that you are looking for an announcer and I'd like to audition."

"Oh, you would, would you?"

"Yes, sir."

"O.K."

Pointing to a table in the room next to the studio, he said, "See the chair and table over there – the one with the microphone sitting on it? Go in there and sit in front of the mike." Then he handed me a copy of the Williamsport Sun-Gazette and said, "I'll be in the studio. When I point to you, start reading."

"What would you like me to read."

"It doesn't matter."

I sat down at the table and unfolded the paper. Dave walked into the studio. He sat at the console, messed around with a tape recorder and pointed. I began reading.

"Just three days ago the Hearst Castle in San Simeon, California was opened to the public for guided tours. Hundreds of people came to see this historic landmark that was designed by architect Julia Morgan as a residence for newspaper magnate William Randolph Hearst, who died in 1951. In 1954 it was designated as a California State Park.

Since that time it has been operated as the Hearst San Simeon State Historical Monument where the estate and its considerable collection of … ."

'Ping, ping, ping.' I looked up to see Mr. Castlebury tapping on the glass and motioning me to come to the studio.

("Oh, great. Well, that was short and sweet. Probably a disaster.")

I stepped into the studio.

Mr. Castlebury extended his right hand. "Congratulations. You're hired."

I was incredulous. "I am?"

"You are."

"Gee ... thanks Mr. Castlebury. When would you like me to start?"

He paused. Then he looked at his watch and said, "Six o'clock."

"Whaaa ... wellll ... Gee ... sure – that's great Mr. Castlebury. Ahmm, you mean, today?"

"Yep. Meet me here around five-thirty. I'll get you started. And call me Dave. You'll be paid the minimum wage to start – $0.85 per hour. That OK?"

A Radio Pronouncer, I

At five-thirty that afternoon Dave took me into the studio and showed me how to operate the console, and get into and out of the ABC Network (WMPT was an affiliate). He also gave me some 3 x 5 cards with the official station breaks.

"I'll stay 'til seven. After that you're on your own 'til nine, when Fred comes in to do 'Night Train'. (Night Train was the nine to midnight show when the station played all the hits for folks our age. Everyone in Lycoming County under age twenty-five listened to Night Train.)

At about two minutes before six Dave handed me a card and said, "Watch the clock. At 5:59:50, open the mic and read this. Then push the network switch down and turn off the mic.

June 6, 1958 @ 5:59:50 PM, I opened the mic and said: "You're listening to WMPT, South Williamsport, Pennsylvania, a service of the Will-Mont Broadcasting Company. Stay tuned for Howard Cosell and 'Speaking Of Sports'."

And that was it. I was officially a Radio Announcer.

The love affair would soon begin.

Ridin' The Wax

I 'rode the board' for a few evenings and weekends, doing station breaks and weather forecasts, and with help from Kerby and Fred I learned which 'pots' were for which channels, how to cue records, how to play taped commercials, etc.

One week later Dave asked me to do a record show – 'Platter Party' – Monday thru Friday, noon to four.

Anyone can learn to cue records, read station breaks and wind a reel of tape onto a tape player. I had no idea what I'd need to know in order to 'present' a four-hour radio program five days per week … and keep it interesting. I wasn't even sure this was possible.

For starters, I decided to leave 'interesting' to the hit records.

Twenty hours every week, playing records and getting paid for it? Heaven. I'm in Heaven.

The following Monday I played my first record on the radio – "I Wonder Why," by Dion and The Belmonts.

I've been wondering why ever since.

No. Really?

In August, Mr. Castlebury informed me that I was to be the football play-by-play man starting in September. Fred Plankenhorn would do color.

Not for one high-school team. For two! Home games only!

I loved football. Per-game pay was $12.50.

"Count me in!"

The South Williamsport Mountaineers played home games on Friday nights. The Warriors of Montoursville played Saturday afternoons.

Our first broadcast was from the Press Box sitting high atop the bleachers at Mountaineer Stadium.

Fred and I arrived at 6:30 to an empty stadium. We climbed the bleachers to the Press Box. The door was padlocked.

We had no key.

Not to worry. The back side of the Press Box was a half-wall only about 3? feet up from the floor, then wide open to the roof's edge.

We decided to 'climb Mt Everest'.

We climbed over the top rail of the bleachers. Then, hanging precariously about thirty feet above the ground, we shimmied over to the open back of the 'box' and hiked ourselves over the short wall into the Box – equipment and all.

If I'd known then what I know now I never would have attempted this.

To paraphrase the late Flip Wilson: "The $12.50 made me do it."

Warrior Field had no Press Box. We just walked to the top of the bleachers, set the equipment on the seat in front of us, hand-held the microphones and did the broadcast – a much safer route to the $12.50.

I was having the time of my life.

By Any Means Necessary

The Bald Eagle-Nittany High School Panthers (BEN – Mill Hall, PA) were an opponent of the Mountaineers. South had a game scheduled at BEN some thirty-two miles away. Because both teams were undefeated, Dave decided to do the broadcast.

Recall that WMPT had only been on the air for about a year. Advertising sales were virtually nil. Monthly station income was near zero.

In order to broadcast the game, Dave would have to come up with money for expenses and for a dedicated telephone from the BEN Stadium to the WMPT transmitter. Cost for the telephone line alone was $50.00, the equivalent of $425.06 in 2018 money.

Out of the question.

What to do, what to do!

"So Dave, can you get me directions to the BEN Stadium?"

"Don't need 'em. We're doing it from the front room."

(In the immortal words of Cochise: "How?")

"So, WBPZ in Lock Haven will be broadcasting the game. I'm going to tune a transistor radio to the station and have a headset plugged into the radio. You'll wear the headset and 'call' the play-by-play of the game based on what the WBPZ announcer says. Should work great."

("I bet!")

"Ahmmm, Dave. This won't sound good without crowd noise."

"Relax. I have a sixteen inch disc of crowd noise that runs at 16 rpm. When you go 'live' with the broadcast I'll start the turntable. When it runs out I'll just lift the needle and start it over."

WBPZ was a 1000 watt station with a primary signal radius of seventeen miles and a 'secondary' of twenty-five. The rocky subsoil in the area served to diminish the signal.

Later that afternoon, sitting in my car in front of our studio, I tuned the car radio to WBPZ, 1230 AM.

The bad news? It was difficult to make out what they were saying.

The even worse news? The static made the above 'nearly impossible' even more difficult.

I had my doubts, but Dave was a technical guy and I wasn't.

That didn't matter. It was too late. I had no choice but to 'go for the $12.50'.

Game Day

So I'm sitting in the same seat in front of the same mic on which I'd done my audition. This time I was 'live and in color'.

Dave turned on the radio and I put on the headsets. The WBPZ announcer began his broadcast.

"Hello footshkans. Welstpsthy hbam Eagle Nittany Pan thersnpfwr iumiaiumhhwhere the v xthscr take on tssht South mthhhshhtvbatr ey nthsthtmmtha. Khlhternoon."

Dave rolled the crowd-noise disc and I began an opening of my own.

OMIGOD! The 'crowd noise' was that of a laid back baseball crowd ... vendor calls, popping cups and the occasional crack of a bat ... with baseball-type cheering.

The jig was officially up.

The WBPZ broadcast continued and I struggled with the re-creation, sometimes calling a game as I imagined it might be.

"Engfhtt olys ... yard line. Firsstpsthy hbam pfwrahh. Olttrqub sshv xthscr South mthhhvbatr ey nmmtha. Lehtcdown. It's 14-7 Bjhytbbshtany."

For two halves of football that's what I heard in the headsets. I got just enough information to make myself believe that what I was saying might sound as if I knew what was happening.

I've no idea what our listener may have been thinking.

I say 'listener' because I never got one single comment about the broadcast – from anyone ... ever.

Maybe only one person was listening!

Or none.

No doubt this was the most bizarre performance of my on-air career.

The Day The Music Died
It's Tuesday, February third 1959 – just after one PM as I recall.

I'm on the air doing Platter Party when I hear the 'bing, bing, bing' of our United Press International News Machine ... the indicator that a major news story was about to move.

I put on a record and went to the machine.

"A plane crash near Clear Lake, Iowa has taken the lives of Buddy Holly, Ritchie Valens and J.P. Richardson."

Wow. This was hard to fathom.

All three of these guys had top selling records. Holly and Valens were loved.

I ripped the story off the wire and read it on the air.

Listeners started calling the station to confirm what they'd heard.

We were in a state of disbelief.

This was a tragedy for the fans of that era ... a huge story.

Here's some stuff that you may not have heard before.

J.P. Richardson was a Dallas Disc Jockey who, as "The Big Bopper" was riding the wave of a huge hit record – 'Chantilly Lace'.

"Hell-ooo BAAA BEE!"

These three men were part of a tour that started in Milwaukee and was playing dates in small cities in Minnesota and Iowa. Most of the musicians were travelling in subfreezing temperatures in unheated buses. Some, including Richardson, were getting sick.

Holly booked the four-seat aircraft to fly to Fargo, North Dakota, where he planned to finally do laundry and rest, in advance of the group's next concert in nearby Moorhead, Minnesota.

Country legend Waylon Jennings, then Holly's bass player in the Crickets, gave up his seat to Richardson in the belief that air travel would afford Richardson a better opportunity to heal. Jennings would be haunted by this decision for years to come.

Dion and the Belmonts were also on the tour, but Dion gave up his seat on the plane after balking at the $36 per seat price tag. He was the only show headliner not on the plane.

Promoters of the show were at a loss about what to do, eventually deciding to employ the services of a band of high-schoolers, well known to the area as being pretty good and featuring a lead singer that teens all over the region knew and loved.

The performance would serve as the 'discovery' of that singer and would lead him to a start-studded career in pop music.

His name?

Bobby Vee.

In 1971 Don MacLean wrote and recorded 'American Pie,' a song that memorialized this tragedy, calling it 'The Day The Music Died'. His recording became a chart-topping #1 hit record that is often played on today's Oldies stations.

Partners

Over the next several months, Kerby and I spent countless hours together at the station. We became good friends and by fall we were partners. We'd made a vow in blood to someday own a radio station together.

We had no earthly idea how to make this happen but we talked about it incessantly.

Presumptuous? Yes, but we never said we were going to own at age 18 – just someday.

We knew there were dues to pay. But we believed.

Seven Days A Week

By fall I was back in school at Lycoming College. Barbie was a high school senior.

I did Platter Party during the week and I signed the station on the air on Saturday mornings. I was also the play-by-play announcer for two local high schools, one played on Friday nights and the other on Saturday afternoons. I was paid a talent fee of $12.50 per game.

Sunday evenings I ran the board for network programming and signed the station off the air at midnight.

I was working fifty to sixty hours per week and earning between $50 and $65 dollars.

Loving every minute.

And I DXed constantly, always listening to the top personalities, trying to learn.

I continued in college through 1959. The busier I was at the station, the better were my college grades. I still haven't figured that one out.

Nirvana

Even though we were very young, Barbie and I were very much in love. We talked about marriage non-stop but she wanted Nursing School. We understood that our marriage would not be happening anytime soon.

Oftentimes we'd be in my car and I'd say, "Hey. Let's run away and get married." Barbie would say, "OK. Let's."

I'd get on Route 15 and head up over the mountain, as if we were running away to get hitched.

I always turned around.

One day we kept going. South. We got married. Shortly thereafter we were expecting.

More Talk

By mid-to-late 1959 our 'blood vow' had become a virtual non-stop conversation. Kerby and I talked constantly about our future partnership as radio station owners. We knew we had lots of growing to do. We had not yet learned about the power gained when one focuses on a specific goal.

We learned a lot about Top Forty Radio from the record promotion men that visited the station, asking us to play their records. RCA's John Rosica and the immortal Matty "The Humdinger" Singer, from Philly.

These guys were constantly telling us about the fabulous salaries being paid to the top personalities in the big cities. We set that as our next goal.

At age eighteen I told Kerby, "If I'm not in a major market by the time I'm twenty-five, I'm getting out of radio."

"Why do you say that?"

"Because there's no way I can raise a family on minimum wage."

Note: From 1959 to 1963, if I said that once, I said it three-hundred times. I was still unaware of the power of goal-setting, but in a rather negative way that's exactly what I was doing. In reality I was really saying, "I'm going to be in a major market by the time I'm twenty five."

Upward Mobility

Sometime in 1959 Matty Singer told me about WSBA, a 5 kilowatt 'flamethrower' in York, PA, doing major-market sounding Top Forty Radio. The station footprint was such that it threw a strong signal, not only over York, but also over Lancaster and Harrisburg, PA. Meaning that the station could be heard by nearly a million people.

WSBA was that regions' only Top 40 station. It was survey-rated the Number One station in all three cities.

Matty said, "WSBA is the jumping-off place. If you can make it to WSBA and do well you can make it to the big time. If you want the big time, get to WSBA."

I knew that York was 130 miles from Williamsport but was totally unaware of WSBA.

It all sounded good to me.

I had no idea of how to get there.

Providence would soon intervene.

Get Outta Town
In the early fall of 1959 Kerb accepted a job at WHGB in Harrisburg. He said he'd be earning $70/week for working forty hours.

A few weeks later he was gone.

Proud Papa
Our daughter was born at 7:09 PM on November 23, 1959. She was a beautiful baby and today she's a beautiful lady. We named her after her Mom.

My Turn

Shortly after New Year's Day, 1960, Kerby called.

"One of our announcers is joining the Army. Come down. Get this job. I'll tell them you're good. It's $65 a week."

I was off to Harrisburg and an interview with Station Manager Ralph Hartman.

I was hired.

Post Script
A sunny, cold day in late January saw Barbie and me and our beautiful baby girl, drivin' down Rt. 15 in our green and white '57 Ford, headed for Harrisburg and our second and third floor apartment at 1840A Park Street.

1840A Park Street,Harrisburg, PA (Image from Google Maps)

I'm the poster child for the positive results attained via the minimum wage.

On day one, at $0.85 per hour, I was overpaid. I knew nothing about being a radio broadcaster. Zero. Nada. Zippo. To Mr. Castlebury the minimum wage provided a low-risk, affordable way to take a chance on me. For me it was an entry into an industry that I would quickly come to know and love, an industry in which I've spent my entire adult life and have prospered in ways that I could never have imagined.

To this very day I often raise a toast to the concept of the minimum wage and what it provided for me.

Hint: Minimum wage is not 'chump change' and it is not meant to be a 'living wage'. It is a stepping stone … paid entry into the work force where an inexperienced person can grab a foothold while getting a free education in what it takes to make businesses and companies prosper, and learning that an outstanding work ethic will quickly lead to higher wages.

CHAPTER FOUR

GATEWAY

Many future major league baseball players plied their minor league trade on the diamond at historic Bowman Field in Williamsport, PA. A large billboard in front of the stadium read, "Welcome to Bowman Field, Gateway to the Majors."

As a kid I loved baseball. I wanted to play in the majors.

I 'adopted' this billboard.

I'd just started my first salaried radio job at WHGB in Harrisburg, PA, on the air Monday thru Saturday nights from 9:00 PM to 1:00 AM. January 1960 found 'Tall Paul Rothfuss' spinning hits for the folks whilst gleaning a cool $ixty-five a week in the bargain.

I was a nineteen year old 'first-full-time-job' radio guy, and a proud husband and father.

I believed I had everything I'd ever need.

Glenda

Evenings at WHGB were an adventure. Barbie was at home with our baby daughter while I shared the company of the vast listening audience in the Harrisburg Metro.

Some of that vast audience? A few folks? A listener or two?

'Twas at WHGB that I discovered my very first 'fan'.

One night I picked up the studio phone and a voice said, "Tall Paul, you is my FAVE-rit Dist Jockey. Will you play a dedication for me?"

"Umm, sure."

"Play 'This Magic Moment,' by the Drifters. Dedicate it to Ricky from Glenda."

"OK. Will do"

"Thank you Tall Paul."

End of conversation.

Thus began a string of 'dedication calls' from Glenda, always with the same opener.

"Tall Paul, you is my FAVE-rit Dist Jockey. Will you play a dedication for me?"

Glenda was an African-American high school girl from Steelton – one of a small handful of our 'regular' listeners. The songs that she requested, and the boys to whom the songs were dedicated, had something in common.

Never the same song – or boy – twice.

Glenda changed boyfriends a lot, but she never changed her FAVE-rit radio station. I always hoped she'd be called by the rating services!

I never met Glenda but I'll never forget her. She was my first 'faithful' listener. At that time probably my only one, but you never know who might be listening.

Something to Aim For

Living in Harrisburg gave me the opportunity to listen to WSBA, 'the jumping-off place',

The station featured 'for-realsie' radio personalities, great sounding commercials, sing-along station jingles, exciting contests, excellent news coverage … all of it. It was a lot like the great stations I heard at night years ago, and like WCAO when I was in college.

Matty Singer was right. WSBA was the hottest Top 40 station in Pennsylvania outside of Philly and Pittsburgh. Just by listening I came to understand how someone who 'made it' at WSBA could then make it to the major markets.

(Would I like to work at WSBA? You bet!)

But to me, getting there was not a consideration. I'd only just arrived at WHGB, beside which was my belief that I wasn't ready to take such a step.

The apartment we rented at 1840-A Park Street was about thirty blocks from downtown Harrisburg and the WHGB studios. Living room and kitchen on the second floor, bedroom on the third. Our telephone was in the living room.

I signed the station off the air at 1 AM every morning, after which I put stuff away and buttoned up the studios, finally arriving home around 2 AM.

Barbie and the baby were usually asleep. Most of the time I got to bed around three and got up around ten.

The Call

One Monday morning, about sixty days after arriving at WHGB: "Honey … Honey. Wake up. You have a phone call."

"Huh … whaa … ahmmm … what time is it?"

"Nine o'clock."

"Who is it?"

"I think he said his name was Sanders."

I stumbled down the stairs and picked up the phone.

"Hullo?"

"Is this Paul Rothfuss of WHGB?"

"Yes sir."

"Thiziz Al Saunders at WSBA. We were in Harrisburg Friday night for the Progress Fire Hall record hop. I heard you on the radio. You have talent."

"Mmffth … th-thank you."

"I'd like you to come to York and talk about joining us here at WSBA. When could you do that?"

"Ahh … mmm … eleven o'clock?"

(Quiet chuckle.) "Well, I didn't mean todaaay. How 'bout Wednesday morning at ten o'clock?"

"Yes, sir – that will be fine, sir. Thank you, sir. I'll see you at ten on Wednesday."

"Great. See you then."

Every time I tell this story I feel the same thrill. It was a life changer.

You never know who might be listening.

The Jumping-Off Place

Wednesday morning, still in a state of disbelief, I started down I-83 to York, PA.

Think of it! Twenty-two months earlier, almost by accident, I'd landed my first radio job. Eight or ten weeks ago I arrived in Harrisburg.

Today I'm en route to 'the jumping-off place'. The Road to the Big Time. WSBA, one of a handful of Pennsylvania's Greatest Radio Stations.

As I drove I tried to prepare myself for the meeting. Everything I knew about Al Saunders I'd gleaned from listening to him on the air. Al had a great voice. He was also very funny.

"You have talent."

He actually said that. I was floored. No one had ever said anything like that to me.

I had zero experience interviewing for a great job like this and I'd never stepped a foot inside a truly great radio station.

WSBA was the flagship station of the Susquehanna Broadcasting Company, the pride and joy of Mr. Louis J. Appell.

I was nineteen. Green as grass and not at all sure I was ready for this giant step forward.

(But wait. Mr. Saunders said he heard me on the air and he liked what he heard. He must think I'm ready. I just have to show him I've a good head on my shoulders. I guess I'll be OK.)

Four Towers of Power
WSBA offices and studios were located at the transmitter site north of York – a large pasture field along I-83 on which sat four tall radio towers and co-occupied by … a herd of Brown Swiss milk cows.

The Four Towers of Power! You couldn't miss this array. Impressive!

I stepped into the front hallway and immediately sensed professionalism. Wow.

(Cute receptionist, right on cue.) "May I help you?"

"I'm here to see Mr. Saunders."

"May I tell him your name, sir?"

(Sir? Really? Sir?)

"Ahhmm … Paul Rothfuss," I stammered.

"I'll get Al for you."

Monogrammed Shirts
I followed Al to his office and sat in the chair facing his desk.

"Hey Paul, thanks for coming down. I'm excited about having you join our staff, which I really hope you will do."

(Where do I sign!)

"I'm the Operations Director at WSBA, and I also do the
Morning Show. As I told you, I heard you on the air on Friday
night. You have talent. I'd like you to join our staff here at
WSBA. Would that be of interest to you?"

I wanted to scream, "YESSSS!" at the top of my lungs.

"Yes sir, Mr. Saunders. Absolutely."

"Call me Al."

(That'd make a great song title, right?)

"Good. For starters I'd want you to work from four to
midnight: On-air with music from four to six and eight to ten,
and on the news desk in between. The pay is eighty-five
dollars a week … is that acceptable?"

I could hardly speak.

"Yes Mr. Saunders. That will be fine."

"Call me Al. Oh, and speaking of names, there's something
else you need to do."

(What? Climb every mountain? Ford every stream? Milk
every cow?)
"Don't take this the wrong way, but you'll have to change
your name. Rothfuss won't make it as a radio name. Nice
German name, but (chortling) on the air it'd sound like your
mouth is full of partly-chewed cabbage."

As he hit me with these words he made a circular motion with his right hand, like it was a helicopter blade. I struggled to hold back a laugh.

"My given name is Alvin L. Steinwedel. Got it?"

"Oh. Ahmm ... yes sir, I got it."

At that Al looked me straight in the eye, leaned forward in his chair and said, "Paul is nice. Keep Paul. I like Paul. And I'd use a last name that starts with 'R' ... you know, Roberts, Robbins, Rodgers? (pause) That way you won't have to change your monogrammed shirts."

(Monogrammed shirts? Are you serious? I don't have any shirts.)

Al did this with an absolutely straight face but inside I know he was laughing his fanny off. He knew the moment was important to me but he couldn't resist having a bit of good-natured fun. That was Al. A sweetheart, but always one funny sumbitch!

First Alias
"I'll go with Paul Roberts." (More on this later.)

"Good choice. So, eighty-five a week, right? I'd like you to start April eighteenth. Can you give notice this afternoon?"

"Yes sir, I can. I'll go straight to the station and tell Mr. Hart- man."

Paul 'Roberts.' May 1960

From C Ball to Triple A

Twenty-two months after my first day on the air I found myself at the radio equivalent of Bowman Field. 'Disguised' as Paul Roberts, I arrived at the Gateway to the Majors.

Friday was payday at WSBA. The first Friday of my employment I opened the envelope that held my check, only to find a mistake.

"Mr. Saunders, there's a mistake in my paycheck."

"Call me Al. So what's the problem?"

"You told me I'd be paid $85 per week. This check is for ninety dollars."

Al quickly replied, "Oh, didn't I tell you?"

"Tell me what?"

"Well, after you left our interview I decided that eighty-five dollars was a little light, so I told the office I hired you for ninety. Is that O K?"

"Ahmm ... well ... yessir, it's wonderful. Thank you."

Shortly after this I became convinced that the payroll snafu was in fact a mistake but that instinctively Al knew two things: One, the extra $5 per week was meaningless to the company but would be meaningful to me. Two, for that five bucks he would absolutely 'own' me, and I'd be loyal forever. He was right.

We never discussed it but I know I have this right.

True confession: Years later, when running my own company, I used Al's 'tactic' a time or two myself.

Lessons
Over the next few weeks I 'got' Al's wry sense of humor. Over the next two years I was the beneficiary of his great generosity.

He taught me everything he knew about how to become a successful radio personality. I sopped it up like the dry sponge that I was.

Al: "Lesson One – Lose the word "I" from your on-air vocabulary. They don't care about what you did. They do care about what they care about.

"What they want from you are indications that you are aware of what they care about. How to get this information? Read magazines and newspapers. Watch local TV. Get involved in the community. Be aware of what's going on."

It was this advice from Al that 'made' my on-air career.

Mr. Saunders

Al had a long and illustrious career. He was a great Morning Man, wildly intelligent and very funny. He was a Program Director, a News Director, an Ops Manager and a Station Manager. And he was a very important mentor to me and many others.

More than anything, Al loved to entertain 'on the radio'.

Al wrapped up his career at a dizzying height. When CNN hit cable TV in 1979, Al was its 'First Voice'. His was the rich baritone we heard on all of the CNN station breaks, promos, program announcements, intros, extros, liners and sweepers.

When Al retired, guess who followed him as the voice of CNN? As if to put an exclamation point on the exceptional nature of Al's work, it was a fella named James Earl Jones.

I'd say Mister Jones landed in exalted company.

Regret

Mine has been a wonderful life. Many blessings. Few regrets.

One regret? I didn't stay in touch with Al. I should have called him at least once a year to thank him for all he had given me. I didn't do that.

If there are people of importance in your life, call them today and thank them.

Al, this chapter is for you. If I get to join you on the other side would'ja consider hiring me again? I promise to bring my monogrammed shirts, and I will call you 'Al'.

CHAPTER FIVE

SUSQUEHANNA | WSBA

Starting Day One at WSBA, Al Saunders was my mentor and teacher. He saw something in me that I could never have found in myself.

His morning show was the best I'd ever heard, a great balance of whacky funny stuff, screwy contests, and 'current' local information, along with outstanding local/regional news coverage provided by Warren Duffy, WSBA's News Director.

In those days, DJs also did news. We were taught to gather and write local news and to re-write the national news off the United Press International news wire that was constantly clacking and printing in the newsroom.

(At last. Value from the eighth-grade-typing class I'd hated.)

The WSBA line-up featured Al Saunders, Wayne Trout, Warren Duffy, Ed Coles, Ed Lincoln, Paul Roberts and Gil David. As a group we were called 'The Sensational Seven'.

Note: Gil David was our all-night guy. "Hey, it's Gil David with Music for the Mushroom People."

Mushroom People?

Oh … Mushrooms grow in the dark. I get it! Clever, right?

I chuckled every time I heard him say it.

WSBA was "Major Market Radio in a Small Market." Everything at WSBA was first class: The best studio equipment, great station 'jingles' created by the Anita Kerr Singers, outstanding commercial production and production aids, top drawer promotion of the personalities including publicity pics and, best of all, great training.

Oh, and we were required to wear dress shirts and ties.

Monograms were optional.

Gil David

Can you say 'thoroughly professional'?

Learning Curve

Al took me under his wing and began to teach. His 'lesson plan' was to meet with me at least once a month and review a tape recording of one of my recent shows – an 'air check'.

Lesson Two: "Paul, you are a very funny guy. Funny is great, but funny is not what gets it done. 'Current' is what matters. You have the talent to 'crack wise' after every record. Not a good idea. How many 'funnies' do you think I do?"

I swear, I thought the answer was 'after every record'. As a listener, that was my perception.

"I dunno Al, three or four an hour?"

"Never more than one, and sometimes none."

(That can't be so. I listen every day. It's at least three.)

"C'mon Al. It's more than that."

He grabbed one of his own air checks. "Let's listen."

The answer was … one.

"If you do too many funnies you become predictable, same as if you never do one. Besides, you'll wear your listeners out. When you think of a 'bit,' write it down for use later. You'll soon have so many you'll never be able to use 'em all.

"Never forget the old showbiz adage: Leave 'em wanting more."

"OK, Al, so what about 'current'?

"Remember Lesson One – losing the word 'I'? The only thing that matters is what they are thinking about, and they really don't care what you are thinking about.

"It's all about you being aware of what's going on in your neighborhood, your community, your area, your country, the world ... and finding ways to let them know that you know ... without ever hitting them over the head.

Your listeners share places with you, so these are their places as well. This is what will be on their minds. See?"

I actually got it. I understood and I began to concentrate on Al's instructions.

SIDEBAR: Have you read Malcolm Galdwell's "Outliers?" Well, this period was an integral part of my 'five-thousand hours'.

By mid-summer Al had rearranged show hours for each DJ. I was given 3 to 7 PM – in radio parlance, 'Afternoon Drive'. The second-most-important 'daypart' on the station.

The Rothfuss/Roberts family moved from Harrisburg to a rented house on Taxville Road.

Beethoven
WSBA's 1960 Christmas Party was underway at a really nice York restaurant.

Barbie and I were proceeding through the receiving line en route to our table. Welcoming us to the party was the owner of Susquehanna Broadcasting, Mr. Louis Appell. Also, Susquehanna's President, Mr. Arthur Carlson, and Mr. Robert Eastman, founder of Eastman Media, a leading rep firm for the broadcasting industry.

Barbie was six-months pregnant with our second child. She always looked beautiful and especially so that evening, wearing her very Christmassy scotch plaid maternity outfit. I wore a sport jacket and slacks with white shirt and tie. No monograms.

The best I had.

Here we were – a couple of nineteen-year-olds about to meet some very important people.

Mr. Appell greeted us warmly, and Mr. Carlson was jocular, as always. As he was shaking my hand he turned to Mr. Eastman and said, "Bob, I want you to meet our afternoon guy, Paul Roberts, and his wife Barbie."

Mr. Eastman said, "It's nice to meet you."

"Thank you, sir. It's nice to meet you, as well."

What followed was totally unplanned.

"Mr. Eastman, may I ask you a question?"

"Certainly."

"If you could sum up in one sentence what it takes to be successful in Top 40 Radio, what would you say?"

Mr. Eastman's reply came back like lightning.

"If Beethoven's Fifth Symphony is the Number One song in the country, introduce it as such and play it every other hour."

There it was: the 'secret' behind the success of Top 40 Radio. Play The Hits … over and over again.

Beautifully explained, don't you think?

TV

Susquehanna also owned a UHF television station – WSBA-TV, Channel 43.

In early August I was chosen to host a teen dance show on Channel 43, sorta like 'American Bandstand, York, PA version'. The show was scheduled for four o'clock Saturday afternoons – talent fee twenty-five dollars. I said "Yes."

(I've no idea whether the show, or I, was any good, or whether anyone was watching. We had fun. I enjoyed the money.)

The Record Promotion men brought recording stars to the show to lip-sync their records just like Dick Clark's American Bandstand. The best to appear on my show was Roy Hamilton, who sang "You Can Have Her." Also Ronnie Savoy with "And The Heavens Cried." Both of these gentlemen were sensational performers.

Charlie McCoy also appeared, doing his hit song, "Cherry Berry Wine." Afterward Charlie came to my house and had dinner with us. Barbie's mom was visiting. Charlie is a nice guy and a great musician. Turns out he's a much-in-demand session guy in Nashville and a Country Music Hall of Fame Inductee.

Next, I was tabbed to record the 'night book' for the TV station … all of the commercials and station breaks that ran from 6 PM to sign-off. This took about a half hour each day and paid another $25.00 weekly. My $90 per week had morphed to $140.00.

Marketing Genius

Shortly after the dance show began I was asked to host a two-hour program each Saturday morning from ten 'til noon … talent fee, $25.

Based solely on the quality of its content, this may have been the worst TV show ever.

But for the show sponsor this was among history's greatest marketing ideas.

In York, a music teacher/entrepreneur had figured it out. I don't remember his name, but he owned a music store and studio selling musical instruments and all the accoutrements: sheet music, pitch pipes, instrument cases, etc., etc.

He also offered music lessons to the budding trumpeters, violinists and accordionists of the area.

This gentleman purchased two hours of Saturday morning TV time, 10 AM to noon. On the show he featured little kiddies (and young teens) playing the instruments that he sold them … his music students using sheet music that he also sold.

Parents and families of these future musical savants thought this was great.

"Hey, Margaret. Little Joanie's gonna be on TV Saturday, playing the clarinet. She's doing so well. Be sure to watch."

And watch they did.

(cue: Yours Truly) – "Next up on our show today, little Mary Epwhissel will be joined by Billy Calooley and Henry Hepstoeten. These cute second-graders will entertain on their violins with their rendition of 'Yankee Doodle'. Take it away."

The screeching and scrawking that followed was unbelievable.

Cats caught in exhaust fan?

Musically this was not good.

But wait!

Mary and Billy and Henry's families thought the kids were great! Those relatives who were unable to be in-studio watched intently at home … and loved it!

For folks whose children had not yet begun their trip to stardom, well, they were going to make darned sure that their kids would soon be on TV as well.

"Marge, call that music studio and sign Katrina up for tuba lessons. I wanna tell everyone she's gonna be on TV!"

Lady of Spain
Here's a little-known fact: It's difficult to tune an accordion. As a result, when two or more accordions play together, they often produce sounds that lie solidly in the 'dissonant' category. A cacophony?

How do I know?

The show featured accordion duets and trios almost every Saturday.

"Next up on today's show, here's Jerry Sulnoster, Kenny Pakken, Lonnie Whaltikket, along with Betty and Letty, the Bophus sisters. These fine fifth graders have warmed up their accordions for 'Darlin' Clementine'. An' ah one, an' a two ..."

By comparison, chalk on blackboard sounded like Wolfgang Amadeus Mozart.

Musically it was brutal. What it really was, was pure Marketing Genius.

PAR III
March 31, 1961 was Good Friday. Oh my, yes.

Ninety minutes after she informed me that she was in labor, Barbie gave birth to our son at the York Hospital at 10:09 AM. We named him after my dad.

Follow Mom's Lead
One sunny April afternoon in 1961, at just before six PM, I came out of the studio to get a drink of water – the fountain being just outside the studio door.

Mr. Carlson's office was at the end of the hall to the left of the studio. The front door was a short walk through the business offices then straight away from the studio to the front door.

As I exited the studio door I saw Mr. Carlson coming toward me, leaving the office for the day. He spotted me and said, "Hey Paul. How're you doing?"

I said, "Fine, Mr. Carlson. But If I have to play that Brenda Lee record one more time I think I'm gonna faint."

Turning left toward the door and without breaking stride he turned his head, raised his arm, pointed his right index finger and said…

"Relax. Mom's just beginning to hum it."

The secret of Top Forty revealed yet again.

First Talent Fee

Chris Huber was a top Media Sales Rep for WSBA.

"Paul, I have a new client in Harrisburg – Doutrich's Men's Store. They want a spokesman to do their commercials and endorse the store. I can get you a talent fee."

Count me in.

Chris and I went to the store and I talked with the manager. He said I could have any suit in the store if I agreed to be their spokesman for one year.

I chose a handsome grey suit with a very thin black stripe. They threw in a couple ties and dress shirts.

For their ad campaign they'd adopted the mantra of every young professional man.

"Doutrich's … for the man who wants to earn $10,000 a year before he's thirty."

In 1961, ten thousand dollars was a handsome sum and an income level to which most young professional men aspired, me among them.

I missed my opportunity to get some monogrammed shirts.

Where's The Can

We were preparing to launch our big summer promotion: "Find the WSBA Water Can."

Check this one out.

We got three of those squareish one-gallon tin cans. We painted 'em white, with "WSBA" in red on both sides.

The idea was to hide one can in the York area, one in Lancaster and one in Harrisburg, then go on the air and give clues to where the cans could be found. A $100 prize awaited the listener who could find the can and bring it to the station.

Find the can. Grab the loot. Easy, Peezie, Lemon Squeezie.

For the location of the Harrisburg can they chose a spot underneath a small bridge over a tiny creek, next to a road that went past the Harrisburg Farm Show arena. I was assigned the task of hiding the can.

Late one night I drove to Harrisburg and placed the can under the bridge, high enough so it couldn't be seen by anyone just driving by, but not so high as to be missed by someone standing at creek level and looking under the bridge.

The contest started. The Lancaster can was found in three days and the York can a week or so later.

The Harrisburg can?

Nada. Nothing. Crickets.

Day after day, clue after clue – no can.

After two weeks we were out of subtle clues and getting desperate. It was almost down to, Go to the Farm Show Arena. A couple blocks up the street is a bridge over a little creek. The can is under that bridge.

Almost.

In the middle of the third week, Al concluded that something must have happened to make the Harrisburg can disappear. I was given one of the returned cans and asked to go up and see if the other can was still there, under the bridge. If not, I was to place the 'substitute' can and scram.

Around one AM I parked the car and walked to the bridge. No sign of the can, but there was a clue.

Have you ever seen a high-water mark left by a flood or a torrent of water from a 'gully-washer' thunderstorm? In my flashlight beam, under the bridge and a few inches higher than where I'd placed the first can, I saw such a watermark.

I put the substitute can there and sped away.

Next morning around ten a listener brought the can to the station and claimed their prize. We announced the winner and the can location, and the contest ended.

Oddly, no listener ever claimed 'foul'. "Hey! I went there a couple of times and I never saw a can. What-the 'H' is going on here?"

And you thought WKRP in Cincinnati's 'Turkey Drop' was history's only Radio Contest Snafu? Not!

President Abraham Lincoln said, "You can fool some of the people all of the time, and all of the people some of the time, but you can't fool all of the people all of the time."

A classic 'some/some' situation.

Post Scripts
Shortly after moving to York I was DXing and re-discovered WCAO, coming in loud and clear from Baltimore. This time around I paid attention with a different, more practiced ear. They still sounded great. WSBA was almost as good.

Toward summer's end, Al asked me if I knew any talented young guys who might be interested in joining the company at WARM, Susquehanna's Scranton/Wilkes-Barre station. By that time, Kerby had left WHGB to be the Program Director at WKVA in Lewistown, PA. Owned by Robert L. Wilson, WKVA was a well-managed small-market radio station known for developing excellent broadcasters.

Kerb and I were always in touch, and while he was happy at WKVA, he understood that a position at Susquehanna Broadcasting would be a big step forward.

I told Al about Kerby.

By September, Kerb was doing Afternoon Drive at the Mighty Five-Ninety.

And I was a farm boy.

CHAPTER SIX

IT'S WARM EVERY DAY

Late summer, 1961. Dad called to say his farmer had been injured and was unable to work. This left him with twenty-five head of Holstein milk cows, fifteen Thoroughbred horses, a busy medical practice, two boys still at home … and no one to do the farm work.

I explained the situation to Al and told him I needed an immediate leave of absence. In early September we moved into the small farmhouse in Nisbet, PA.

Dad hadn't seen the kids in a couple of months. When he saw our son he went four-alarm. "What's wrong with the baby?"

"I don't know, Dad. He's growing longer but he's not gaining weight. The pediatrician keeps telling Barbie to "… give him time."

"Time, hell. The time is now. I'll call Dr. Blumberg and we'll get to the bottom of this, and I mean now."

The next day Barbie and the baby went to Dr. B's office with Dad. The two doctors examined the baby and had some blood drawn for analysis. Our son was anemic to the max, a continuation of which would have resulted in disaster.

Within two weeks he blossomed.

Note: I'm convinced that this move 'home' saved our son's life.

Alone

Dairy farming is the hardest work I've ever done. It's relentless. Every twelve hours the cows must be milked, the operative words being every and must.

And dairy farming during cold winters in North Central Pennsylvania is brutal.

Especially when it's just you.

I got along great with the animals, but cleaning up the dairy barn? Yeeeckh!

Any thoughts of ever becoming a dairy farmer froze to death that January.

Lesson? Learning what you don't want to do is very important.

Relief

In early March of 1962 Kerby called. "We need you at WARM." I headed for Scranton to meet the Station Manager.

In April of 1962 I rejoined Susquehanna, this time at WARM – "The Mighty Five-Ninety." My salary was $125.00 per week.

We moved into a wonderful first-floor apartment at 1755 Adams Avenue in Dunmore, just off Electric Avenue. Mr. Flynn was our landlord and a fine man was he.

Mighty Indeed!

Susquehanna owned powerful radio stations with big coverage areas – large footprints. To take advantage of this the company developed and perfected a marketing strategy they called 'strip-marketing'.

For on-air identification purposes they ignored the radio station's City Of License. Instead, they chose identifying words mirroring the total footprint of the station. In other words, the entire listening area of the station, the 'marketing area,' became its 'location'.

WARM broadcast with 5 kw at 590 on the AM dial. This huge footprint covered all of Lackawanna and Luzerne Counties, and most of the rest of Northeastern Pennsylvania.

Susquehanna renamed the market 'WARMLand'.

Other than the FCC-required top-of-the-hour station identification we never said 'WARM in Scranton'.

It was always 'In WARMLand'.

We gave specific town locations for events, news stories, etc., but we never said "… here in Scranton" or "… here in Wilkes-Barre." Instead it was, "We're live from the Fireman's Carnival at the Olyphant Fire Company, in the middle of WARMLand."

Brilliant!

Together Again
Kerb and I were reunited, this time as experienced professionals
- Paul Roberts, noon to four and Kerby Scott, four to seven.

Quarterly Hooper Radio Ratings showed us with a 53.9-share of the 12+audience from noon to six PM Monday thru Friday.

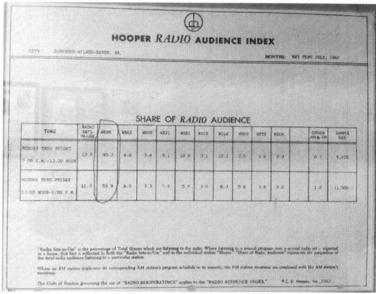

A Fifty-three Point Nine Share!

WARM had more listeners than the rest of the thirty stations in our footprint – Combined!

No radio station will ever again see ratings like that.

Crowds
And could we ever draw a crowd!

The annual WARM Day celebration was set for July at Rocky Glen Park.

Record Promotion Men arranged for twenty-seven acts to appear on the Rocky Glen stage, located at the bottom of a large natural amphitheater.

Yep. Twenty-seven acts! And the show was free.

The Dovells with "Bristol Stomp," Brian Hyland with "Sealed With A Kiss," Bobby Gregg with "The Jam," The Orlons with "South Street," and Bobby Vinton with the #1 smash hit song on the Billboard Magazine charts – "Roses Are Red."

Twenty-thousand people showed up, rockin' out on a hot summer night.

Woodstock before Woodstock. But not nearly as messy!

Tim-Berrrr!

The Sensational Seven hosted. Harry West, Don Stevens, Paul Roberts, Kerby Scott, Ron Allen, Len Woloson and Tommy Woods. Our news guys were there as well: Terry McNulty and Jerry Dyer.

The stage floor was maybe ten or twelve feet above ground level, at the bottom of the amphitheater.

Standing on the stage at six feet tall, my eyes were eighteen feet above ground level, so if I looked straight ahead I would be seeing folks who were sitting or standing a good distance up the hill.

A few large hardwood trees were scattered around the hill. Guys climbed these trees to get a better view of the action.

I was standing stage right, looking into a huge crowd that was really into the music. Directly in front of me some fifty feet away was a tree, in a crotch of which was the right foot of a guy.

The dude was holding on to the tree with his right hand whilst attempting to perfect the new dance he was inventing – The Left Arm, Left Leg "Look Mom" Twist.

For a minute or more I watched him twisting – wild-eyed, with two left limbs flapping about. Then, perhaps overcome by euphoria, his right leg emerged from the crotch of the tree and joined his left limbs, leaving only his right arm to secure his position.

For a precious few seconds I observed the most macabre set of dance moves ever witnessed, and then …

… he was gone!

He'd lost his grip and fallen, fifteen feet to the ground. I thought, "He's gotta be out cold."

But no!

He bounced up, brushed himself off, re-climbed the tree …

… and kept on rockin'!

I assumed this was all done without the aid of any chemical stimulation.

Truly a mighty listener to a Mighty Radio Station.

Carlson One More Time

One day while listening to a distant station, I heard a jock do a bit that I liked. I changed it up a little and, early one afternoon, I did it on my show.

En route to Scranton, Mr. Carlson was listening.

Sometime after two the studio door opened. Carlson stuck his head in the door and said, "Hey Paul, I heard that bit you did awhile ago. It was good."

"Thank you."

"Did you make that up?"

Red faced, I said, "Ummm, nawhh."

"Where did you get it?"

"I, err, I ahh … kinda stole it."

"Do you do that often?"

Still chagrined, "Not too often. Once in a while."

Carlson smiled. "Good. Always remember – if you do something like that once, it's stealing. If you do it more than once – that's research."

Door closed.

Carlson gone.

Note

Arthur W. Carlson was a great broadcast executive. I learned a lot at Susquehanna, both from Mr. Carlson and from the top people he employed.

By the way, the writers of "WKRP in Cincinnati" modeled the role of the station manager after Carlson. Gave the character his name, too … played by the late Gordon Jump.

'WKRP' got it almost perfect. Right down to the va-voomski receptionist! But they did get one thing wrong. Stuff that happened in one episode actually took about a week to happen in a real radio station!

BTW: At most radio stations there's only one person who knows everything that's going on.

The receptionist!

Major Marketitis

Scranton is close enough to New York and Philly that we could hear the top radio personalities there. I may have been delusional, but the more I listened the more I believed that I was ready for that next step – the jump to the Major Leagues.

And my old mantra resurfaced. "If I'm not in a major market by the time I'm twenty-five, I'm getting out of radio." I was twenty-two.

Kerb and I talked incessantly about working in bigger markets. By December of '62 I was ready for my own version of Chairman Mao's 'Great Leap Forward'.

I'm not naturally a good networker. Other than the record promotion men and the folks at Susquehanna, I knew no one in the industry. Ergo, attempting any such 'leap' would have me in the role of the Lone Ranger – sans Tonto.

SIDEBAR: Years later I became enamored with a fabulous lecture on the vital nature of goal setting. In 'The Strangest Secret' Earl Nightingale proclaims: 'After a person commits to a goal they will automatically begin to make decisions necessary to reach that goal'. While this advice may seem to make no sense, it was nevertheless to be accepted on faith. Mr. Nightingale assured that this would happen. With none of this as prior knowledge, I was about to put his advice into play.

Decision Day

Via repetition of my 'major market' mantra I had (unwittingly) chosen a goal. Automatically, good decisions started to fall into place.

Never having done so I was unsure of the process re: contacting other stations about employment. I assumed it started with the Program Director, but which stations should I approach?

Baltimore was the only major market with which I was even slightly familiar. I liked Baltimore, mostly because I'd been there with my Dad many times. And I was somewhat familiar with WCAO because I'd spent so many hours listening.

What the heck. Baltimore it is!

In January of '63 I decided to apply for a position at WCAO.

I 'scoped' one of my air checks, packaged it with a letter of introduction, and mailed it to: Mr. Larry Monroe, Program Director, WCAO, 1102 North Charles Street, Baltimore, Maryland.

Weeks passed. No response.

While I never expected Mr. Monroe to be in a mad rush to contact me, I did expect some kind of acknowledgement that he'd received my package.

"Hey Kid. I got your tape. You stink. Stay in Scranton."

Even that would have been sufficient.

But silence? I thought that was unacceptable.

Chutzpah Meets Shock

I'm not a person who looks to 'get up in someone's face,' but by the end of January I'd 'taken it personal'. I was insulted.

Using what might easily have turned out to be the worst possible timing, I screwed up my courage around 4:40 on a Friday afternoon, and I called WCAO.

"WCAO. Larry Monroe."

(The Program Director answering the phones? Impossible!)

I don't remember how but I was able to say, "Ahhhm, Mr. Monroe, this is Paul Roberts from WARM in Scranton, PA."

"Hold on a sec. I'm on the air."

Radio patter, then, "Yes, Paul. I got your tape. Not only that, I've heard you on the air."

Totally unexpected.

"Really?"

"Yeah. We were in Pittston a few months back, trying to buy a radio station. You have talent."

"Thank you, sir. I'd like to talk to you about coming to work at WCAO."

"That might be OK, but I don't have any openings."

"Yes sir, but I didn't ask you if you had an opening. I said I wanted to talk with you about working at WCAO. People leave radio stations all the time, so you never know when you'll need someone."

(Note: This is one of the brashest things I'd ever said to anyone. I've no idea where it came from … not Paul. In retrospect, it sounded like something I'd never say.)

What followed was amazing.

"When will you be in Baltimore?"

"Tomorrow."

(Not true right then at 4:45 that afternoon. By 5 PM it was true.)

"Great. Be at the station at ten o'clock. We're at 1102 N. Charles Street."

"Thank you, sir."

"See you tomorrow."

How Bizarre

Making the call was gutsy. Mr. Monroe answering the phone was unlikely. What transpired was absolutely impossible.

I called Barbie.

"Honey, I have an appointment in Baltimore tomorrow morning at ten – at WCAO. I'll be home at seven. Have the kids ready to leave."

A few minutes later she called back. "We'll drive to Harrisburg and stay with Jim (her brother). You can go to Baltimore in the morning."

Barbie has always been right there, the finest life partner any man could ever have.

Big B
So … my second 'big job' interview.

Wait. There's no job, right?

At ten AM sharp I met Larry Monroe in the lobby at WCAO.

He showed me around the studios, the newsroom and the control room. At WCAO the DJs didn't spin the records or play commercials. That was done by engineers at the controls in a room on the other side of a triple-glassed soundproof window. This was all very new to me.

We went to Larry's office where he invited me to have a seat.

"Let's listen to your tape."

Larry pulled open the bottom drawer of a metal file cabinet where I saw – ulp! – at least fifty reels of audio tape … in serious disarray.

They all looked the same – brown audiotape tightly wound on clear plastic reels. I thought, "… and they probably sound the same, too."

Each of these tapes had been sent to Larry by DJs looking for work at WCAO.

He wound my tape thru the heads of a small table model Wollensack reel-to-reel tape recorder and hit 'Play'. "Paul Roberts on WARM" flowed from the speaker. I sat there, insides churning. I never enjoyed listening to my air checks. Still don't.

After a few minutes Larry hit the 'Stop' button.

"As I said yesterday, you have talent. But I don't have anything available."

"Yes sir, I know. But I wanted to meet you and personally tell you I want to come to work for you at WCAO. You never know when you might need somebody."

Larry thanked me for coming and we said our goodbyes.

I was back in Scranton by seven.

Ides (Or Thereabouts)
March in northeast Pennsylvania offers few sunny days.

'Twas on a cloudy late March day that I learned the sun can shine anytime … sometimes when you least expect it.

We worked a six-day week at WARM. Monday through Friday it was "The Paul Roberts Show" from noon to four, home for dinner four to five, then back to the station to do news from five to seven. Sundays, records from noon to four.

In our apartment, a long hallway led from the kitchen to the front door. On a table in the hallway sat our white Princess phone.

(Historical note: In lieu of an ugly black dialer you could have a petite white Princess Phone for an extra $0.50 per month.)

I was breezin' down the hall after dinner, headin' back to the station to do some news, when the Princess rang. I picked her up.

"Hello."

"Paul. Larry Monroe. I want you to come work for me at WCAO. Starting pay is $125 a week with built-in increases. Be in Baltimore Saturday around ten and I'll give you the details, OK?"

Somehow I mouthed a muffled, "OK. Sure."

I was stunned. And thrilled beyond measure.

Saturday morning I met Larry. He explained the job and my hours and asked when I could start. I told him I'd try for mid-April.

I flew Cloud Nine back to Scranton, called my General Manager, went to his house and resigned.

I was on my way to the Big Time.

Alias #2

"You'll have to change your name."

Larry said I'd be replacing a guy named Rob Roberts who had been asked to leave under unfavorable circumstances.

"How about 'Paul Rodgers'?"

(Are you kidding? I'll be Paul Rinnabisaki if that's what you want.)

"OK with me."

(I so very much wanted to add, "That way I won't have to change my monogrammed shirts." I resisted. Larry wouldn't have gotten it anyway. You had to be there!)

Welcome Aboard?

Next stop was the General Mangers office where Larry took me for an introduction. There, sitting in a big chair behind a gigantic desk, was a rather small man.

We walked to the front of the desk and Larry said, "Bernie, I want to introduce you to Paul Rodgers, our new DJ."

Without standing, the GM gave me a two-second dismissive glance, extended his hand across the desk and growled, "Nice ta meet-cha, kid. Don't send out the laundry."

And went back to his paperwork. A real confidence builder, yes?

As I was about to leave Larry said, "By the way, you'll be required to join AFTRA."

(Hell, I'd join the French Foreign Legion if that's what it took to work here.)

What's AFTRA?

Retroesque
Looking back, I came to the conclusion that mine was probably not the most impressive audition tape in Larry's file drawer.

I did have enough talent to be hireable, but more importantly, I was the one person who'd gone out of his way to show interest in working at WCAO. By so doing, I'd saved Larry many hours of listening to audition tapes and contacting people.

Note: When applying for a job, you must first understand that labor is a commodity. There are many people who can do that job, some of whom are 'better' than you.

So what is it that will make you 'stand out' from the rest? This is why a personal interview is a necessity.

Movin' Up
On April 10, 1963 Barbie and our two children arrived from Dunmore to our rented row house on Marlora Road in Baltimore. The van arrived shortly thereafter.

On Monday, April 15, 1963, 'disguised' as Paul Rodgers, I made my debut on WCAO – doing news from 4 to 10 PM and music from ten to midnight.

Paul Rodgers has been my professional name since then.

Our Baltimore adventure was underway.

CHAPTER SEVEN

CALLED UP

My impression of unions was generally unfavorable. At age twenty-two I believed they held back individual initiative in order to protect workers that could not (or would not) keep pace.

Truth? I had no experience with unions and had no idea what to expect.

I called my Dad to get his thoughts.

"Dad. In order to work at WCAO I have to join the union."

"So? Join the union. But on payday be sure to note who signed the check."

This was in line with another of Dad's great lessons. "When you're working for someone, behave as though you own it."

Thanks Dad ... I got it.

Note: Adopting this attitude would lead to one of the finest compliments I ever received.

Landing

I arrived in Baltimore on a Sunday night in mid-April, 1963. I was not due at the station until four PM on Monday, but I went in early to get organized and meet the rest of the staff.

Starting with Morning Drive, the line-up was: Steve Wade, Alan Field, Les Alexander, Larry Monroe, Johnny Dark, Paul Rodgers, and Jack Edwards. Frank Luber was the News Director and worked mornings. I did news from four to ten PM, and records from ten to midnight. I started that very Monday.

A year or two later our staff was enhanced by the presence of a talented young newsman named Alan Berrier, later to appear as 'The Bear' on a popular morning radio show in Baltimore.

At this writing, Frank Luber is a friend of 50+ years and sharp as ever. He's still active in Baltimore as a Morning Host on All-Talk WCBM. He's been on the air in Baltimore for nearly sixty years and favored me by writing the Introduction for this book.

My pal, Alan Berrier, is the proprietor of the Bluestone Restaurant in Timonium, one of Baltimore's finest restaurants.

Frank and Alan are great friends today and two of the finest men I've ever had the pleasure to know.

Show Me The Money

The moving van was due to arrive on Wednesday. Cost for the move was around $400.00. I wasn't close to having the full amount, but I got an idea about where to get it … and this is where you learn of my deep abiding love for, and familiarity with, Thoroughbred horses.

Early that Tuesday morning, with nothing to do until four PM, I went to Laurel Race Track in Laurel, Maryland where Dad had a horse in training. I checked in with the trainer, Fred T. Wright, and hung around with him for the morning.

Around eleven o'clock Fred and I were in the track kitchen having an early lunch. Fred's nose was buried in The Daily Racing Form, checking the entries for the day.

"Look here, Paul. Remember that colt your Dad sold awhile back – Gain A' Friend? He's in the third race today."

"I remember … a skinny little colt. We called him 'Archie'. Guess I'll stay around and watch him run."

Fred gave me his paper and I moseyed over to the Clubhouse to watch the first couple of races.

(I learned to read the Racing Form when I was eight years old. To the uninitiated the Form reads like hieroglyphics. To me it was 'Jack and Jill'.

Winner!
My recollection is that I had seventeen dollars in my pocket as I perused the first two races.

(What-the-hell. $13 is about the same as $17 so I-got-nothin'ta-lose.)

I picked the one-horse in the first race and bet $2 to win. Then I picked the three-horse in the second race and bought a $2 Daily Double ticket, the one with the three.

"Annnd They're Off!"

Wow! The one-horse wins the first race and pays $18. Recap: I now have $31.00 in my pocket and I'm 'alive' in the Double.

Feeling my oats (pun intended) I bet another deuce on the three-horse to win in the second race and he's ten-to-one!

OmiGod!

The three wins the second race and pays $22, and the Double pays $346.00.
$$\$29 + \$22 + \$346 = \$397.00.$$

("I'm rich!")

A wave of relief washed over me. I had parlayed my $17.00 stake into moving money ... almost $400.00.

Stay or Walk Away
If there's a "one-to-ten" scale for risk-takers I'm a definite ten.

The third race was fifteen minutes to post and Gain A' Friend was 12-1. My handicapping made him a solid shot to win.

For a brief moment I considered the wonderfulness of cashing a $20 win ticket on a 12-1 shot.

This was quickly followed by a 'thought balloon' – the mind-picture of me explaining to the moving truck driver that I didn't have enough money to pay him, and him telling me he was leaving with our furniture.

I decided to leave.

My car was in the barn area. From the Clubhouse I had to walk the 'wrong way' of the home stretch to get to the barn – track on my right, viewing stands on my left. With just a few minutes to post I started toward my car.

"They're Off!"

I stopped and stood at the rail where the horses would soon come out of the turn and head for home.

And here they came.

Horses breathing hard. Whips popping, hooves pounding. Jocks smooching and whistling. Clods of dirt flying everywhere as the field headed toward the wire.

I watched, and from a distance I thought old 'Archie' was the winner.

Race Results

In 1963 Thoroughbred racing was a very popular sport, so the daily newspapers carried the daily entries and previous day's charts.

Next morning I picked up a copy of the late lamented Baltimore News-American. Sure 'nuff, Gain A' Friend won the race and paid twenty-six dollars and change. A $20 bet would have netted me another $260.00 payoff.

No matter. I had what I needed.

The van arrived around eleven, the movers unloaded our furniture and I paid them in full. In cash.

Barbie and I unpacked some stuff.

Around three PM I kissed 'em all and headed for the station.

The Neon Lights Are Bright

In baseball parlance I'd made it to 'The Show'.

Baltimore is a major market. WCAO was Baltimore's runaway Number One rated radio station and a Top Forty Legend.

I was 22 and had achieved my goal of making it to a major market before I was 25.

We were together – Barbie, the kids, and me.

Life was good.

Working nights provided me with lots of time for my family. My daughter was 3? and my son was 2 so school was not an issue.

Barbie and I loved (and love) the countryside of Baltimore County. We're traditionalists so we adored the quaint farm sites, many of which featured ancient, beautiful stone houses, many over 100 years old.

We put lots of miles on our 1962 Mercury Comet station wagon, driving aimlessly about, dreaming of living in the County. By the end of June we'd made it a goal to someday buy a place in the country.

It happened way sooner than anticipated.

One lovely July day we found ourselves on Tracey's Road, just off Yeoho Road. A cute little house was for sale. The sign read "Gladys R. Nest, Realtor."

We wrote down the phone number and headed home.

Later that afternoon, a call to Mrs. Nest revealed the listed property to be a three bedroom rancher on a slab, with three-quarters of an acre of ground. Ponies in a field behind the property.

Adorable. Perfect. Asking price, $17,900.00.

We made an appointment to see it.

We'd found our first home.

The Laundry Be Damned!

A few months of listening to Baltimore radio had me convinced that I belonged, that if I lost my job at WCAO I was good enough to find employment at another Baltimore station. Plus, Washington, DC was just down the road and they had radio stations too.

I never thought of myself as the best thing on the air but I absolutely knew I was as good as most, and better than some of the rest.

And I knew my work ethic was second to none.

This realization enabled me to quickly get over the very chilly reception I'd received from WCAO's General Manager a few short weeks back.

Note: His admonition, 'Don't send out the laundry,' came from baseball. Major League Managers said this to rookies who'd just arrived from the minors.

"Don't send out yer laundry kid. If ya can't hit the curveball yu'll be gone before it's done."

I sent out the laundry and we bought the house for $17,500.00.

I remember driving away from our closing at Progress Federal Savings & Loan.

"My God, honey, we owe that bank fourteen-thousand dollars."

Our monthly house payment was one-oh-nine and change.

We moved in September first ... to the little house on Tracey's Road in Sparks, Maryland.

Ten days later, Barbie told me she was pregnant.

Workin' Nights

Both rating services, Hooper and Pulse, listed WCAO as the Number One Rated station in Baltimore. Top hit music, an outstanding news presence, great DJs, whacky contests, phones ringing off the hook.

1960s Top Forty Radio. On steroids.

My ten-to-midnight two hour show was, without doubt, the least important spot on the station.

I read top-of-the-hour news for Johnny Dark from 6 to 10. He did the same for me until midnight. Jack Edwards would arrive around eleven to prep for his all-night show.

Note: The most important spot was Morning Drive, typically five to nine or six to ten AM. This was the cornerstone day-part on which the rest of the station was built. A good morning show generally led to listener retention the rest of the day.

Fire In The News

We read the news standing in front of a mike that was mounted on a six-foot stand ... one minute headlines on the half hour, three minutes of news on the hour.

The UPI newswire teletype ran twenty-four/seven printing news, sports, whatever ... on a never ending roll of yellow paper, ten inches wide and however long it was when you ripped it off the printer. (Inside the studio we referred to this as 'rip-n-read' news.)

One night I stepped to the mike to read the news, three feet of UPI paper hanging from my hands.

As I started reading the news over the fading intro music, Johnny Dark came over with his cigarette lighter and, from the bottom, lit the paper on fire.

I proceeded to read history's fastest/shortest newscast.

Funny guy, that Johnny Dark.

The lesson?

Newsprint burns faster than I can read!

CBS, November 23, 1963

At just before one PM I was sitting on our living room couch, changing my shoes, getting ready for a late lunch. It took about forty minutes to drive to the station. I liked to leave around three. The TV was on, tuned to what I can't recall.

"This is Walter Cronkite reporting for CBS News. President John F Kennedy has been shot."

The rest is a blur.

I left at once for the station. WCAO dropped all music programming to carry only network news about this terrible event. We stayed with full news coverage for the remainder of the week.

I worked the news desk the following Friday afternoon and evening. Sometime in the evening the UPI News bell went off, signaling that something special was about to move on the wire. I went to the teletype machine.

Using only numbers, letters and spaces, a clever news writer 'typed' an amazing portrait of JFK.

When it finished printing, I tore it from the wire and hung it on a peg on the newsroom wall. The following Monday it was still on the peg.

I removed it and took it home.

I still have this unique work of art – a 'picture' of our fallen President, created with a typewriter by a UPI news typist using only numbers, letters and spaces.

Genius I say.

Upward Mobility

Around ten-thirty on an early December night in 1963, Larry Monroe came into the studio when I was on the air.

He'd never done this before. I was a bit nonplussed.

What happened next about knocked me to the floor.

"I'm not pleased with our morning show. Starting Monday I want you to be my morning guy."

(Whaaat? Mornings?)

I was speechless. Flabbergasted.

"Me? Mornings? Ahh, geez Larry, I'm not sure I'm ready for that."

"Oh, you're ready. Trust me. So?"

"Yeah. Well … sure, OK Larry. If that's what you want. I'm flattered. And also scared to death."

"Relax. You'll be fine. You have talent."

(Morning Drive on Baltimore's Number One Station. Me? My God.)

Post Script

Many years later (in my late fifties) in a conversation about my time on the air in Baltimore, I offhandedly said, "Yeah, I was the Morning Man on Baltimore's Number One station when I was twenty-three."

Those words took me aback. While the statement was true, I'd never looked at it that directly before.

In retrospect, yeah, this was pretty wonderful stuff.

Never having done mornings before, I couldn't wait to see how this was gonna work.

I was about to find out.

CHAPTER EIGHT

RADIO BALTIMORE | WCAO

Larry Monroe arrived at the station every morning around 8:45.

He'd walk through the facility shaking hands and greeting everyone who was aboard, always ending in the studio where I got a big handshake and an enthusiastic "Hey Paul. Great show this morning."

(Not every day Larry. Not every day.)

Kerb Calling

On a chilly late-February morning in 1964, Larry came in the studio and sat down.

"Paul, I need a new guy to do nights. D'ya know anyone?"

Shortly after I got to Baltimore in '63, Kerby called to say he'd landed his 'dream job'. He would be the Program Director at WOLF, the top-rated station in Syracuse, NY. He went on and on about the job and all the perks he was promised.

This was what he'd always wanted so it sounded great to me.

I hadn't spoken with Kerb in many months. In early '64 I assumed things were hunky-dory.

"Geez, Larry, right off the top of my head I can't think of anyone."

"OK. Let me know if you do."

Unbelievable

Around five-thirty that afternoon I'm in our kitchen, warming up after shoveling snow. Barbie is preparing dinner. The phone rings.

"Paul. It's Kerb."

"Hey man, what's up?"

"It's a disaster."

Kerby spent the next few minutes telling me the all-too-familiar story of deals changed and promises broken. Nothing new here. Written contracts with disc jockeys were rare so they tended to get jerked around a lot.

"It's a mess. I gotta get outta here."

"You're not gonna believe this. This morning my PD asked if I knew anyone who was good and might be looking. I thought of you but then I told him 'no'. Last time we talked you were doin' great in Syracuse."

"I'm leaving for Baltimore. See you in the morning."

"Larry Monroe is our PD. Can't wait ta see ya!"

Guess Who

Next morning Larry arrived right on time, but this time he had company.

"Hey, Paul. Sounding good today. Look who I found."

And Kerby stepped into the studio!

With wintry weather the entire way and few interstate highways between Syracuse and Baltimore, Kerb drove all night. He was waiting in the lobby when Larry arrived.

"Ya think he's pretty good, right?"

"Oh yeah."

Larry hired Kerby on the spot.

Two weeks later Kerb and I were making history again, this time at a serious major-market radio station.

April 7
It's really dark at four AM but I was awake, getting ready to go to the station.

Barbie stepped into the hallway. "Baby's coming."

I was galvanized into action.

Our first child was born less than two hours after Barbie began labor. Our second child arrived even more quickly.

Both times we lived just a few minutes from the hospital. This time Mercy Hospital was in downtown Baltimore some fifty minutes away.

"Gotta go – now!"

I was terrified.

Barbie?

Unperturbed.

Within ten minutes we were under way, arriving at Mercy Hospital around five-twenty.

I explained the urgency to the admitting nurse who whisked Barbie away, then I called the station around 5:30.

"WCAO – Jack Edwards."

"Jack. It's Paul. I'm at Mercy Hospital. Barbie's having the baby. I won't be in this morning."

Call to Jack around 6:15.

"Jack, it's a boy. See you about seven."

We named our second son after my college roommate.

The Liverpool Hour – A Star Is Born
Kerby's arrival and my move to mornings enabled Larry to change the on-air lineup. Larry came off the air to be a full-time PD. I was on from six to ten AM, followed by Alan Field, then Les Alexander.

Johnny Dark moved up to afternoon drive – 3 to 7 PM. Kerb was on from 7 to midnight and Jack Edwards continued as our 'All-Night Satellite'.

The 'British Invasion' was in its early stages. My ever-prescient partner had an idea.

The 'new sound' of the English groups was filling the Top 40 charts. The young crowd was eating it up.

Kerby suggested putting an hour aside for nothing but English music.

"How about 7 to 8 PM, Monday thru Friday? We'll call it The Liverpool Hour."

Larry agreed.

'The Liverpool Hour' debuted in April of 1964.

It was an instant Smash Hit!

The Beatles phenomenon started the insanity. This quickly morphed to where, regardless of their music, any British guys with English accents, long hair, and a record were immediately adored by hordes of American teens, mostly girls.

How else to explain Manfred Mann or Freddie and The Dreamers?

Kerby Scott became Baltimore's official Liverpool Disc Jockey. This was big, and it was about to explode!

SIDEBAR: Baltimore was always a 'soul music' town and that never changed. The British Invasion was unstoppable, but rather than totally giving in to the 'hype', our listeners simply broadened their musical tastes.

Our charts always had a few less 'invasion songs' than were found on the charts of stations in other markets. Soul music remained king in Big B.

Pirates
Shortly after the start of TLH, Kerb got in touch with an English DJ named Terry.

Here's Kerby's description of how this transpired.

So we made contact with Terry, a DJ on "Radio Caroline," the 'pirate radio' ship anchored in the English Channel. Terry suggested a record exchange.

We would give them advance DJ copies of new US 'soul music' releases and they'd give us advance copies of new British releases. Being able to 'break' the newest American music gave Caroline a huge advantage over the staid BBC. In return, WCAO got a huge jump on its competition by playing the latest British music first, ofttimes before the records were available for sale. (The record companies hated this!)

It worked great! Radio Caroline crushed the BBC in the London ratings. They were seen as very 'hip' and way ahead of the curve while the BBC came off as 'nowhere'. (This was documented in a 2009 movie, "Pirate Radio," starring Philip Seymour Hoffman.) Meanwhile, WCAO was crushing its competitors.

I was never shown the ratings in Baltimore, but I was told it was the first time WCAO had ever beaten Oriole baseball, and that we were even rated #2 in Washington DC.

I'll never forget opening that first box from "Caroline." Inside were the first releases by Tom Jones, Petula Clark and the Rolling Stones.

In Baltimore 'The Liverpool Hour' led the British Invasion.

Uh Oh
(Feel free to use your best British accent here.)

"I say old boy, we have a problem."

Kerby's coif of choice was a buzz cut. He looked like he'd just mustered out of the Marine Corps. Decidedly not 'de rigueur' amongst the Mods, who were busily adopting the hairstyles of the British cats.

Meanwhile, the Liverpool Hour buzz was deafening and I had an idea.

(short version)

"Hey Kerb," sez I. "Get with it, man. You can't be the O-Fishull Liverpool Jock whilst sporting a United States Marine haircut. Kerb, you need to grow your hair long."

"I'd never do that."

"Ya' gotta."

"Won't happen. Not gonna do it."

"Oh, yeah? Well I think I can make you do it."

"Howyagonnadothat?"

"I'm gonna get thousands and thousands of signatures on petitions. Then you'll be forced into it. Are you ready?

"Here's the deal.

"I'll go on the air and tell listeners that you're a chicken because you won't grow your hair long like the Beatles.

"You go on your show and say you're not gonna do it.

"I repeat the challenge and you continue to refuse.

"After a week or ten days, I'll ask listeners to send me signed petitions demanding hair growth. I'll tell them you agreed to do it if we could get ten-thousand signatures.

"Whadda ya think?"

"OK. If you can get the petitions, I'll do it."

(The 'long version' involves a lot more convincing that had to be done, but you get the idea.)

Next morning I went on a couple of on-air rants about Kerby's short hair.

"Hey gang, have ya seen Kerby Scott? He's all about this Liverpool Hour thing but he's a phony. Are you kidding? With that buzz cut?

"Come on man. He needs to grow his hair long, like the Beatles ... get with the program, know what I mean?"

He goes on his show that evening with, "I heard what Rodgers said this morning. Nope. Not gonna do it."

Phones ring off the hook as we go back and forth like this for a week or so. Then I tell 'em, "Kerby Scott says he won't grow his hair long. Let's make him do it!"

"Here's the deal gang. Get a bunch of petitions circulating around school, work, the office ... wherever. If we can get lots of petitions we'll win.

"Get after it! Circulate those petitions. Get everyone to sign 'em, then send 'em to me, Paul Rodgers, here at WCAO."

Kerby goes on his show. "Petitions? Never gonna happen. No one cares about my hair."

BAM-O! Envelopes come pouring in – by the dozens! Thousands of signatures. Ten-thousand? Hell, we doubled that. Easy.

Kerby caved … sorta. He agreed to let his hair grow long if I would shave my head.

"Deal," sez I.

And He Never Thanked Me

Kerby (Confer) Scott

Kerb's first 'haired' public appearance came when he and I introduced the Dave Clark Five at Baltimore's Civic Center. Thirteen-thousand screaming teenaged (mostly) girls were in attendance.

Ya' shoulda heard the noise when Kerby walked on stage.

Pure pandemonium.

We created a monster.

I made him a star!

Pie

I love slapstick humor. I'd always wanted to take a pie-in-the-face in front of a crowd. (Weird, right?)

The Dave Clark Five show offered me that chance.

I went to a bakery and bought a nice fat chocolate pie.

Before the show, I got with Kerb who agreed to the following: We'd go out on stage and fake a short argument about his hair – Kerby angry with me for 'making him do it'. Me defending myself with, 'Hey, don't blame me, (gesturing to the crowd). Blame them! They're the ones that made ya do it."

Then he hits me with, "Yeah, but you said you'd shave your head ... and you didn't. I owe you one!"

We'd go back and forth a couple of times until, finally, he reaches into the box, withdraws the pie, and SPLOSH! He hits me in the face.

Well ... it went off like clockwork. When Kerby smeared me with the chocolate pie it was the loudest laugh I ever heard!

Did we love this?

In the words of the immortal Little Beaver, "You bet'chum, Red Ryder."

HEAD FULL OF PIE FOR AN UNSHAVEN HEAD was the fate of Paul Rogers, one of the WCAO Good Guys announcers of the Baltimore radio station of Plough Broadcasting, Co. Seated with him are other Good Guys Kerby Scott, Les Alenzander and Frank Luber. WCAO'S Good Guys and the famed Dave Clark Five (in back row) had the Baltimore Civic Center swingin' with an all-day promotion as a thrilling climax of the Revlon Swingstakes Contest. During the show Good Guy Scott wowed the audience by socking Rodgers with the pie because Rodgers didn't keep his promise to have his head shaved while Scott grew a Rolling Stone hair-do. As You can see, Scott (sitting next to Rodgers) let his hair grow wild.

SIDEBAR: Prior to this show I didn't realize the 'pies' the Three Stooges and Soupy Sales used were made of shaving cream!

We got chocolate pie on the huge red draw-curtains that adorned the Civic Center Stage.

Those folks were maaaad!

But hey, we were just two fresh-faced Pennsylvania boys trying to earn a living.

Whoops
Sometime in late April I received an invitation from the Ford Motor Company.

Along with fifty+ morning DJs from America's best stations, I was asked to come to Detroit for the official debut of the new Ford LTD sedan. (From Baltimore: Perry Andrews, WBAL; Lee Case, WCBM; Joe Knight, WFBR, and yours truly representing WCAO.)

The long weekend would feature a stay at a top hotel, a superb banquet with entertainment by the Serendipity Singers ("Don't Let The Rain Come Down"), and a day at the Ford Motor Company track to test-drive the LTD.

The idea was for us to get familiar with the LTD so we could go on the air with ad libbed 'endorsement' commercials for the car.

As payment we'd get the use of a new LTD for one year.

We were a one car family living in the country. I gratefully accepted the invite.

A few days later came the big announcement: The Beatles would play the Baltimore Civic Center in September of '64. Naturally, WCAO would be the 'sponsoring' radio station.

This would occur the same weekend as my 'free car' trip to Detroit.

What to do, what to do.

On stage with the Beatles, ("The fans will remember them, and couldn't care less who else was there … and it's a freebie appearance") …

… or a new LTD for a year.

Mine was steel blue with a silver roof. A lovely car.

CHAPTER EIGHT–A

THE EMPEROR RISES

The whacky stuff that began with Top Forty Radio in the '50s and '60s served as inspiration for the hit TV show, "WKRP in Cincinnati." The writers and producers did a nice job, but not in their wildest dreams could they have equaled the crazed reality that was radio of that era.

Here's one for you.

Emperor Hudson

Bob Hudson was a wildly creative, totally nutzo LA disc jockey who, on a whim, declared himself "Emperor of Los Angeles." (See what I mean?)

Hudson went all out for this one.

He created a complete package, including costuming, customized on-air jingles, wallet-sized membership cards (sequentially numbered for contesting), newspaper and billboard ad templates, promo announcements, etc. Everything needed for a successful radio promotion.

No element of 'crazy' was omitted.

One morning 'Emperor Hudson' appeared on KRLA. The City of Angels went nuts.

Listeners fell all over themselves getting cards so they could be one of Hudson's Commandos and win prizes.

Hudson was all over Southern California 'in costume' with his entourage of Commandos and scantily clad harem girls.

He dreamed up 'missions' for his Commandos, suggesting they take over San Francisco, cover it with water and make it the world's largest ice skating rink, or advocating the straightening of Sunset Boulevard to create the world's longest bowling alley.

This went on for months. Hudson's ratings went through the roof.

KRLA was thrilled.

Hudson was too. So much so that he syndicated the package.

In March of 1964, WCAO purchased Bob Hudson's Emperor package.

Sidebar
In 1971, Bob Hudson and fellow DJ, Ron Landry, recorded "Ajax Liquor Store." It's a scream.

"Ajax Liquor Store"
http://emperorrodgers.com/Chap08a-1.mp3

This record could not be made today. It makes fun of drunks.

It's funny as hell!

"Ajax Liquor Store" was a charted hit record that served as impetus for several comedy albums recorded by these two goony-birds.

Emperor Rodgers, 1964

One March morning I stepped out of the studio to find Promotions Director, Wilma Clark, waiting for me.

"Hey Paul, guess what? You're The Emperor."

"Huh?"

"Don't ask. We need to get started."

I'd been shanghaied. Co-opted. Elevated and Coronated. I loved it!

Wilma and I proceeded to go over the Hudson package, getting familiar with what we'd need to roll this baby out. Photo shoots, newspaper and billboard ads, bus sides, wallet-sized cards, Commando certificates.

And a costume.

I decided on a royal purple tunic awash with gold fringe, a crown of grapes, and gold caligae (heavy-soled sandals) with attached leather thongs that wrapped my calves.

Chic, don't you think? (I still have the costume, and I'll wear it at book signings if our readers demand it.)

A few weeks later the station broke the news.

Emperor Rodgers was in control!

The Rush To Enlist
WCAO had a big footprint and a huge listening audience.

From Bel Air to Annapolis, from Maryland's Eastern Shore to Frederick, Rodger's Royal Commandos arrived from all directions. High school and college age folks joined the ranks in droves – both boys and girls.

Within a matter of weeks we had over 20,000 wallet cards in circulation and we were giving away stuff like mad.

The Official Rodger's Royal Commandos Membership Card.

And Mail

My oh my did we get mail, much more stuff than we could ever keep.

Each morning I saluted responders by name, giving them on-air shout-outs and inviting them to the next planned (faux) event.

Things like turning the Loch Raven Reservoir into a giant strawberry milk shake, or the upcoming Gladiator Games pitting Rodger's Royal Commandos against the Baltimore Colts football team. Thank God this never happened!

But you get the idea.

All of this triggered suggestions from Commandos themselves, which served to keep the craziness fresh.

First Pitch

The Orioles asked me to!

Yes. On a soft summer evening, Emperor Rodgers took the mound at Memorial Stadium to throw out the first pitch at a Baltimore Orioles game.

I was announced to the crowd and escorted to the pitcher's mound. To my surprise, I found myself accompanied by two young musicians wrapped in bed sheets (togas?) and blowing herald trumpets. You know … those long straight ones from the King Arthur movies?

Here's the first-hand scoop from one of those trumpeters:

Don and I played in a Baltimore R&B band that occasionally worked the dances and pool parties hosted by radio jocks. Through this connection we got the call to herald in Emperor Rodgers for his pitching debut. I suspect the musicians' union would have considered us 'scabs,' but for us it was a golden reward for all those trumpet and trombone lessons.

Ted's Music Store on E. Centre St., still a Baltimore icon, was the place to go to rent a herald trumpet – essentially a brass pipe with a mouthpiece on one end and a flared bell on the other. White sheets served as togas, and with no sandals available we went barefoot.

This was a combo thrill of inside baseball and grand theatre that was pretty exciting for a 17 year old. More than my appearance before the crowd, I was super excited just to be in the dugout while waiting to be announced. There they were … right there behind me … 'real' baseball players, warmed up and in uniform … revered icons … and, as I was soon to learn, huge assholes.

What else would you call a man who would hock a giant nicotine-laden loogie and aim it at an innocent young boy's bare foot, (with pinpoint accuracy, I might add)?

I shook it off and we walked out there blowing some sort of bugle call on those horns.

The crowd cheered, the Emperor threw the ball, and we left through the dugout … but my clearest memory of that day, to this day, is that Oriole ball player spitting his nasty-ass tobacco juice on my foot.

My wind-up started well but the kick wreaked havoc. The caliga on my left foot caught the edge of the pitching rubber and I almost went down.

The pitch was low and way inside.

My major league dreams were forever crushed on that mound … with me dressed in a purple tunic. Embarrassing!

Lesson?

Don't play baseball wearing caligae.

Nexxxt!

Dr. Arthur Watson was Director of the Baltimore Zoo. He hosted a one-hour program Sunday mornings on WCAO where he talked about 'everything zoo'. He was a true friend of the radio station.

Wilma asked him if we could 'borrow' a lion. He said yes!

At around 11:30 on a weekday morning in June or July, draped in purple tunic with gold-fringe tassels, gold sandals, and wearing his gilded 'crown of grapes', Emperor Rodgers and his entourage of scantily clad slave girls appeared in Baltimore's main downtown shopping district.

I mean – right downtown amongst the office buildings, the jewelry stores, the banks, the exclusive ladies and men's clothing stores, the restaurants, and the big fancy department stores like Hutzler's, The Hecht Company and Hochschild-Kohn.

(Have you no shame?)

The streets were crowded with shoppers and office workers going to lunch. Our intent was to get noticed.

Hey … timing is everything, right?

Folks were astonished when we appeared, probably because one of the harem girls was 'walking' a lion on a long gold chain.

A large tawny American mountain lion.

Old. Perhaps toothless. But a lion nonetheless.

For about an hour we went up and down the street smiling, waving, and handing out Commando Membership Cards.

(In my mind I'm in a D-grade, pseudo-Cecil B. DeMille movie.)

Nuts-O? Did we get noticed? This was 1960s Top 40 radio at its whacky best. Stuff like this was going on all over America.

I was just a fresh-faced Pennsylvania boy trying to earn a living.

SIDEBAR: We later learned that 'Leo' had been given a light pre-appearance tranny. Whew!

You'd never be permitted to do fun stuff like this today. The 'fear of deathers' have successfully choked the humor out of nearly everything.

And PETA? The mere thought of this would have them twisted up like pretzels.

Then again, was there potential for an actual living, breathing lion breaking bad in a crowded urban shopping district?

Maybe we *were* nuts.

Speaking Of Mail – The 'Real' Military

Two Plebes at the US Naval Academy in Annapolis, MD started their own 'chapter' of Rodger's Royal Commandos by 'enlisting' many of their fellow cadets and (presumably) their girlfriends.

Note how they carefully worded their 'enlistment' to reflect that the Naval Academy was in no way connected to or involved with the Commandos.

I've always wondered how things turned out for these fine young men and women.

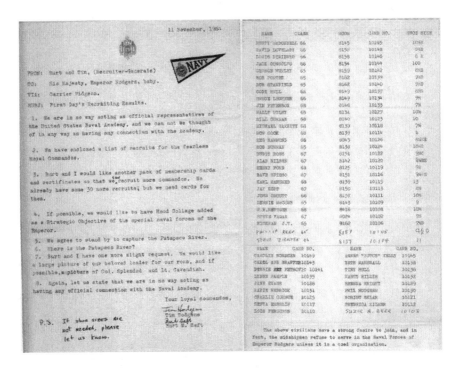

We received stuff like this in the mail nearly every day.

Now it's December, 1964.

In the mail arrives a missive from none other than …

King August I

Wild and crazy it was. And clever. And creative. And funny as hell.

Somebody put a world of time into this. I guessed this was a high school boy.

Using his wonderful imagination and artistic talent he'd created his own 'kingdom' and carefully prepared it for a merger with Rodger's Royal Commandos.

On the air 'The Emperor' officially welcomed the King and his Kingdom into the fold.

Another envelope arrived with even more great stuff.

I saved it all.

It's impossible for me to adequately describe this so I'll let the King speak for himself.

August I
Ave, August

YOU'RE INVITED

VERITAS EST VEENUM

Rex Worldum
Morituri Te salutamus

‡B‡O‡R‡K‡B‡O‡R‡K‡B‡O‡R‡K‡B‡O‡R‡K‡B‡O‡R‡K‡B‡O‡R‡K‡B‡O‡R‡K‡B‡O‡R‡K‡B‡O‡R‡K‡B‡O‡R‡K‡

Dear Emperor Rodgers,

The IMPERIAL Government of King August I, ruler of the World and Beyond cordially extends to you this IMPERIAL Invitation to attend the "Convention of all Emperors, Kings, and Dog Catchers of the Universe and all which surrounds It" being held this year right here on Earth in the IMPERIAL Castle, "Mount Ribbley-on-the-Jerome", of August I, who is the Secretary P.F.C. of the convention. Your presents are requested (we also want you to come) and these topics will be discussed thereat: (1) who will have possession of the quazzi tree next tenure; (2) consideration of deporting carbonated bork juice to other parts of the Universe; (3) will Emperors and Kings be able to serve as disc-jockeys in their spare time; (4) and various and sundry other topics important to peace in the Universe.

Present will be such famous-all-over-the-Universe personalities as Emperor Erick von Sterick of the planet Quazzi (that's where August got the quazzi trees), and King Fergunw X. from the planets Ferggw and Krudw (he's known for the silent w's on the end of all his words).

You will have as your official personal translator and beautician Sir Derfy Pedderdorf, known the Universe over for his translations and beauty.

Please inform us of your decision so that we may prepare a seat for you in our most IMPERIAL Convention Hallway, thank you.

Love,
August I

August I, King

Sir Derfy Pedderdorf

Sir Derfy Pedderdorf, P.M.

P.S. We forgot to tell you the date of the convention.

Dear Emperor Rodgers,

    The IMPERIAL Government of August I, ruler of the World and Beyond, is hereby returning the results of your entrance exam and it has been found you are one of the three persons to pass this difficult test (the other two being August I, and Derfy Fedderdorf, the makers of the test). It is fortunate for you that our skilled scholars were listening to your program when you answered the test orally and though you got a perfect score we had to subtract 1.4% because you answered the test orally and didn't send us the written answer sheet, thus giving you the only passing score of 98.6%. Herewith is mailed the remainder of the kit of the "August I College Completion Course in One Easy Lesson". If you satisfactorally pass this prufung you will be sent your PhD (fudd) degree.

           Love,

          August I

          August I, King

          Sr. Derfy Fedderdorf

          Derfy Fedderdorf (Sir that is), P.M.

          Burby Cubble

          Burby Cubble, Chairman Board of Examiners

P.S. Don't forget to pay your bill, 8,000,000,000 Idiot Head 3¢ pieces and the township of Dorchester County, as it is due the first of the month and if you don't pay we will have you thrown into a debtors' prison. And we will!!!

jlhmlv:jlh

I never knew the identity of King August I. I always assumed he was a high school student, and it was obvious to me that he was a talented graphic artist and a person who had a 'way' with the English language, especially where humor was concerned. The secret was safe for fifty-three years ... until I started this book. [see 'Epilogue' for an amazing King August update!]

JUST BECAUSE He's LATe
DON'T THINK KING
August, the

KIND, Benevo-
LeNT, Modest,
Charitable,
UNSElfish, good
NATURED, Loving

benign, sympathetic, warm
hearted, Sweet-Hearted, Amiable,
Tender-loving, friendly, Tolerant,
considerable, merciful, good
Samaritanical, bearer of good-
will, well wisher (he wishes you had a well)
and sweet; wishes you
A Merry Christmas
!!! ...

Hee Haw

In April of 1965 we got a request from the Severna Park High School PTA.

"We'd like it a lot if the WCAO DJs would help us with our fundraiser by playing our faculty in a game of Donkey Basketball."

Our Program Director immediately agreed.

We were now committed to another rare opportunity – an entirely new way to make asses of ourselves. To accomplish that, we joined forces with some real asses.

Worked like a charm!

———

Here's one reason why America is such a great place? There are so many unimaginable and creative ways to make a living.

So ... the PTA had engaged the services of a guy who went all over the country 'renting donkeys'. The donkeys resided in an old school bus, the interior of which had been converted into a sort of rolling stable.

(I thought of this as 'exchanging one set of asses for another'. But I digress.)

On the night of the game I got a tour of the facility and an explanation from The Donkey Meister.

"I'm on the road from mid-March through October, going from town to town providing the donkeys for sporting events like this. My fee is a percentage of the gate – usually half."

See what I mean about 'creative'?

"All my donkeys are broken to ride but several are trained to do funny things."

"What might that be?"

"That's a trade secret. You select your donkey at random. You'll discover their special skill when the game starts."

The Emperor Selects A Steed

In full Emperor regalia, I selected a donkey and walked him – it? – to center court with the other nine 'players'. We were instructed to mount up and play basketball as if there were no donkeys involved.

Dribble the ball, pass the ball, shoot the ball. You know … play basketball.

The two teams mounted up. The referee appeared, blew his whistle and tossed up the ball.

Chaos ensued!

Some of the donkeys followed the steering commands of their riders so something remotely resembling a basketball game broke out. Well, sort of.

Mine?

Not!

He stood quietly as I got on board, but each time I urged him onward he went to his knees, lowered his head, and I slid down his neck to the floor.

Four or five times! (I'm a slow learner.)

Another donkey walked along quite nicely when being led, but when the rider climbed aboard the donkey stood absolutely still – like a statue. He simply would not move under any circumstances.

Another donkey would only back up. Still another would move out from under the rider each time he attempted to mount.

And another had only one gait. Trot!

At any given time there'd be five to seven donkeys 'playing basketball' while three or four others misbehaved as they'd been trained to do.

Picture this: Five donkeys moving up and down the court, each with a rider on their back attempting to dribble (and occasionally shoot) a basketball, all of them weaving in and out amongst a standing-still donkey ..,

... a donkey moving aimlessly about as his rider attempts to mount,

... a donkey 'in reverse' with rider aboard,

... a donkey trotting around and around with the rider onboard and helpless in his attempts to get the beast under control,

... and a donkey slipping the rider down his neck.

Caught you laughing, didn't I!

Enter The Tactician

Fifteen or sixteen donkeys were available, but only ten were on the court at any given time. At halftime, the Donkey Meister ran them all together for a new 'random select'.

For the second half I drew a donkey that behaved.

One of the teachers drew 'The Statue'.

When he realized his donkey could be led but would not move when he got on board, the teacher led the donkey to the WCAO defensive basket, stationed him on the right side at 'layup distance,' climbed on board and called for the ball.

Each time this teacher received and controlled a pass he'd make a 'chippy'.

Can you say, "Leading Scorer?"

The Severna Park Faculty routed the WCAO Good Guys.

The place was packed to the rafters and the gym roared with laughter. The home team fans loved it. The PTA said, "We should do this again next year."

We didn't.

NOTE: All over the USA, through the late fifties and sixties, Top Forty Radio Stations and Disc Jockeys were doing stuff like this. And worse!

Hey! Just tryin' to make a living!

Hubris

As a fundraiser, this was a wonderful success. Apparently the word got out because other PTAs began calling the station to schedule 'normal' hoops games – their faculties vs. the WCAO Good Guys.

Our Program Director served as the 'coach', which was interesting because he couldn't play worth a damn. (Those who can, do ... those who can't, coach?)

Plus, we didn't have enough DJs to field a complete team, and most of the ones we did have, stunk. 'Ringers' were called in to help. We had some really good ones, too. The Baltimore Colts' Andy Nelson and Willie Richardson played frequently (both were really good). Former NBA Baltimore Bullets player, Walt Budko, played occasionally. And we had a couple of 'friends' who also helped out.

———

Our Program Director lost his mind and began scheduling five to seven games each month. They even got a Volkswagen van to carry us around. It was ridiculous.

This was supposed to be a fun thing for the spectators – rooting for their faculty heroes (good players) as they torched the 'famous' WCAO Good Guys (bozos – not much basketball talent). Not hard for us to lose, even when we played our best. Besides, without 'letting them win' we really needed to lose. For public relations reasons if nothing else.

Problem was, the PD got the bit in his mouth and insisted that we go all out to win every game, which we could do on many nights when the Ringers showed up. You know, when the WCAO DJs (the guys that folks came to see) sat on the bench most of the time?

My Game Day Schedule: Get to WCAO by 11 AM. On-the-air from 3 to 7 PM. Leave on the 'Team Bus' at 7:05 PM. Game over around 9:30PM. Home between 10:30 and 11.

I started opting out of most of these events. As a family man working a six-day week, I began to resent this claim on my family time. Soon it became clear that the PD was torqued when I chose not to play.

I could not have cared less.

The fun and games had been turned into 'For-Realsie Basketball' followed by guys going out for beers. Not for me, and certainly not five to seven nights each month.

Note: 'Trying to win' led to a series of very unfortunate on-court incidents, always because the competition got out of hand. Really bad PR for WCAO.

Problem? The PD was behaving as though this all mattered. His hubris was showing.

Eventually we'd played so often that the uniqueness became commonplace – it wasn't 'special' any longer. We'd killed the goose that laid the golden egg.

In 1967 the air was let out of the WCAO basketball for good.

"Red Auerbach, Jr.'s" career as a basketball coach was over.

Whew!

The Donkey Ball Team Photo

STANDING–WCAO TEAM, L to R: Jack Edwards (DJ), Alan Field (DJ), Nick Zaharis (Sales Dept.– coach), Walt Budko (ringer/former NBA Baltimore Bullets), Johnny Dark (DJ), Les Alexander (DJ), Frank Luber (DJ), Paul "Emperor" Rodgers (DJ).
KNEELING–HOST TEAM: Our opposition, whose names I don't know.
SEATED–WCAO CHEERLEADERS, L to R: Staff Person (?), Sylvia Butts (Traffic Manager), Rosemary ? (Secretary).

Hannibull

March, 1965. The Ringling Bros. and Barnum and Bailey Circus is making its annual appearance in Baltimore.

The circus train always arrived at Penn Station on North Charles Street, where circus personnel disembarked from the railcars and formed an old-timey circus parade, clowns and aerialists walking – the Ringmaster, too.

Lions and tigers and bears in decorated wheeled cages.

Equine performers mounted on their steeds, on their camels … and on a zebra.

Vendors.

More clowns.

Led by the elephants, the parade would make its way down Maryland Avenue to Baltimore Street and the Civic Center, where the circus was to perform.

A typical parade day saw hundreds of people lining Maryland Avenue, or watching from office and apartment windows high above the street, cheering as the circus parade passed.

This year, Emperor Rodgers was the Grand Marshall of the Circus Parade.

Riding down Maryland Avenue.

On an elephant.

In near-freezing weather.

Wearing only a purple tunic.

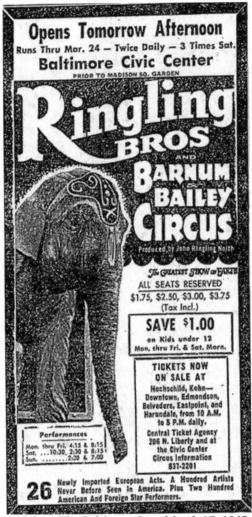

Ad from The Baltimore Sun, March 17, 1965

Up You Go

This was not a nice March day in Baltimore. This March day was cloudy and blustery, and a not-so-balmy 43 degrees.

The Emperor, dressed in his afore-described tunic, is to mount the lead elephant and lead the parade down Maryland Avenue.

Mount? ... The elephant?

I envisioned an elephant-shoulder-high ladder leaning on the beast. Or perhaps the handler would cup his hands into which I'd put a foot, then he'd boost me up to scramble aboard. I don't know ... a cherry picker?

So, "Howinthehelldoyougetuponanelephant?

Here's how.

The handler approaches 'Jumbo' from the left side and pats him on the head. In response, Jumbo kneels and sort of tucks his head. The top of his head is now five or six feet off the ground.

In the process of kneeling, 'Big J' bends his leg into a position where the rider can use the 'knee' like a step stool, grab the strap around Jumbo's neck, and pull himself up the last three feet to the elephant's head – facing backwards.

I'm on board and 'J' (by now we're BFFs so I call him by his nickname) – 'J' is asked to stand. I do a spin move to get facing in the right direction.

And off we go.

(Note: That was when I was twenty-four and agile. Today we'd be calling in the cherry picker.)

Up A Hill — Down A Hill
We headed out from the train station, up a small rise on Maryland Avenue, then down a small hill and up another slight rise to where I could see the harbor area dead ahead.

Very quickly, the wind turned into a nasty, cold, biting adversary, the buildings forming a sort of funnel, forcing the wind to blow across the Emperor's bare legs and up his skirt … er, tunic.

In less than five minutes, every part of me not touching elephant was frozen.

———

The parade reached the summit and started down the final hill, with the Civic Center still many blocks below.

Many, many, frigid, teeth-chattering blocks.

Straight downhill we went … into the wind.

Wfheewfheerfwheeerwheeeeee. (That's the sound of cold wind blowing up an Imperial tunic.)

Here I was … on an elephant. Freezing to death.

And I thought of Hannibal.

You know: The Roman General who took elephants over the Alps?

At the start his army numbered 38,000 infantry, 8,000 cavalry, and 38 elephants.

We know that nearly all the elephants perished on the journey. There's no record of any of the soldiers writing about this trip. Did they all freeze to death?

Maybe. I believed I was going to!

And what of the Cheering Throngs?

A few faces peered down from the warmth of their upper-floor digs but no one watched from the street – it was too damn cold.

Baltimoreans are too smart to stand outside in that kind of weather. They wouldn't even do that if they could stand next to a nice warm elephant. Maybe Johnny Unitas, but an elephant? Not!

It took forty-five minutes for us to reach the Civic Center.

It took me an hour to thaw out.

And two weeks to be totally free of the elephant smell.

My, my my … they are pungent behemoths.

Lessons Learned?
1. It doesn't snow on the Serengeti.
2. 'Bummer' events often create oddly pleasant memories.
3. Elephants have a 'musky' odor that lingers. It's a gift they readily share with all who choose to ride them.
4. Five to seven days of constant attention to personal hygiene will eventually result in the elimination of most elephant odor … the operative words being 'eventually' and 'most'.

CHAPTER NINE

BALTIMORE JAM

I was a night person, so life as a Morning Man had its drawbacks for me.

Getting up for work at 4 AM, taking a 'nap' from 2 to 3 PM, then staying up 'til midnight for Johnny Carson … it just wasn't working.

My post-afternoon nap 'grouchy' was beginning to wear on Barbie and the children.

Not good.

Barbie and I talked about this often. I needed to have my work schedule changed. I had no clue how to make this happen.

In April of 1965, Larry Monroe left WCAO to manage a radio station that he purchased in Pennsylvania, near Pittsburgh. Our new PD was Bill Sanders, who joined the staff from a station in Albany, NY.

This happened about the same time I'd made up my mind to go to Larry and ask to change my on-air time, perhaps to afternoon drive. Now it would be Bill I'd have to confront.

Not the best way to start with a PD who'd only been there for a week or two.

Today's The Day

When Bill arrived at the station he stopped by the studio first.

"Hey Paul. G'morning. Sounding great."

Larry redux?

On this day I responded with, "Thanks Bill. Hey ... d'ya have five minutes for me when I get off the air?"

"Sure. See ya at ten."

———

A few minutes after ten I screwed up my courage and went to Bill's office.

"Hey, Paul, have a seat. I know you wanted to talk with me, but before you start there's something I gotta tell you.

"The home office called yesterday and told me they wanted me to go back on the air. Please – don't take this the wrong way – we think you're doing a great job. But when Bill Sanders is on the air, Bill Sanders does mornings.

"Starting Monday I'll be doing mornings. I want you to move to afternoon drive.

"Whaddya think?"

(Pinch me! This is a dream, right? Stuff like this never happens. Or does it?)

"Ahmmm, well ... sure, Bill. Yeah, that's fine with me. Yeah. Whatever you want."

(Incredible.)

"Good, thanks. Now whaddya have for me?"

"Ohhh, nothing. A question about an entry on the program log. Got the answer."

I was knocked out. I'd gotten exactly what I wanted (and needed) with no instigation from me. None at all.

The following Monday I began an eight-year run. Afternoon Drive on Baltimore Radio – four years on WCAO and four more on WCBM.

Takin' Baltimore home from work was the best part of my on-air career.

—————

So there we were. Back to back – again

I was on from three to seven and Kerby from 7 to midnight.

Just like the old days!

Eudowood

I met Marty Resnick when I was doing a record hop in east Baltimore. I believe the hall was owned by Marty's father, but Marty was the manager. He had an open Friday night on his calendar and rather than let the place stand empty, Marty decided to try a record hop – his first effort in that genre.

Marty had contacted Kerby, who was unable to do the hop because he was on the air on Friday nights. Kerb put Marty and me together. Marty and I hit it off and the Friday night dances began.

Because he'd provided the contact, I suggested to Kerb that we 'partner up'. He'd promote the event on his show and I'd appear and MC. We'd split the fee.

We had a great crowd.

At the same time Marty was preparing to open a hall of his own, Martin's Eudowood Gardens, at the Eudowood Plaza in Towson. That first record hop was successful enough to convince Marty that he should book hops at Eudowood every Friday night. Marty proposed a partnership.

Marty would supply the venue and Kerby and I would promote the event on the air and run the dance. Our wives would work admissions and collect the money.

We'd have a live band every Friday and we'd hire a couple off-duty Baltimore County Police Officers to 'hang around,' just in case. Proceeds and expenses were split three ways.

With the combination of great local bands, great records and contests, and superb promotion on Baltimore's #1 Station we knocked it out of the park, routinely drawing four to six-hundred teens to our dances.

Kerb and I always worked very well together.

The best was yet to come.

Soul Men

Baltimore had lots of really good bands, made up mostly of high school and college age people. I mean lots of good bands.

The Admirals, Tommy Vann and the Echoes, The Majestics, Denny and the Hitch-Hikers, The Princetons, Bob Brady and the Concords, The Dynamics, and on and on.

And from Washington, DC, The El Corols, featuring the El Corolettes and El Cyd.

The Majestics (circa 1966)

L-R, Kneeling: Larry Schumache-alto sax, Duke Gore-bass. L-R, Standing: Ray DeMoss-tenor sax, Frank Invernizzi-piano, Jim Cosby-trumpet, Don Lehnhoff-trombone, Bill Whitelock-drums, Rex Little-trumpet, Bob Sutton-guitar, Denny Picasso-vocals. (Note: Don Lehnhoff is the guy who 'took a loogie' before trumpeting the Emperor to the mound at Memorial Stadium.)

These bands had a lot in common. All had full horn sections – trombones, trumpets and saxophones – and most had an organ player (1965 terminology. Today, a keyboard player).

Their stock in trade? 'Covering' the hit soul sounds of the day. Otis Redding, Sam and Dave, James Brown, Ray Charles, The Temptations, Wilson Pickett, Rufus Thomas, Percy Sledge, and so many more.

These young instrumentalists were talented, well trained and dedicated. They were beautifully rehearsed. They all featured really good lead singers.

Had they been in Baltimore, any recording star with a hit on Motown, Stax/Volt, or Atlantic Records would have heard their songs covered 'live' at the record hops and dances. They would have been impressed.

Mitch Ryder certainly was.

Yes, that Mitch Ryder. (More to follow.)

One or another of these really good bands played 'live' at our dances every week (typically from 8 to 11 PM, mostly on Friday nights). I spun records and had contests during the band breaks.

Our dances were the place to be.

We packed 'em in.

The Yardbirds
The British Invasion was in full swing and English groups were touring North America.

The Yardbirds were set to play a large venue in Montreal but the date was cancelled when an uprising caused the government to call up the RCMP. Their next gig was in Washington, DC, about a week hence, meaning they had nothing to do for several days.

Somehow, their manager knew about The Liverpool Hour. He called Kerb and asked if he'd like to have the Yardbirds play a gig free of charge.

Yes. Free of Charge.

The catch? The appearance had to be on the forthcoming Friday night, just five days away.

"Marty, we can get The Yardbirds for a Friday night live appearance. For free. I bet we could get over a thousand kids for that. Are you 'up' for it?"

"Who are The Yardbirds?"

(Beautiful.)

"A British group with a big hit record."

"Do it."

We already had The Admirals booked – one of Baltimore's very best bands. This Friday was going to be a monster.

———

The building was 'fire-scaled' for 625 people. 1,100 joined us.

The stage floor was about four and one half feet above the ground floor. Anyone standing 'up front' needed only to reach out a hand to touch any musician who ventured close to the front of the stage.

When The Admirals were on, the crowd was spread over the entire area. Ya need room to dance, right?

From my vantage point on the stage it appeared as though the room was chock full o'people.

I took the stage to introduce the Yardbirds and the crowd formed a half-moon shaped 'crush' in front of the stage. I was amazed to see the amount of 'empty space' at the back of the room.

The Yardbirds featured Jeff Beck, Keith Relf and a couple guys who later formed Led Zeppelin. At the time we didn't realize how good they really were.

Can you stand it?

Long hair and all, The Yardbirds played for about fifty minutes. Lots of applauding, some screaming, and some other (obligatory) crowd noises followed.

The crowd loved every minute ... but there were no 'incidents'.

Nobody grabbed anyone. No one rushed the stage.

Quiet it was not.

Peaceful it was.

Thankfully.

Could you do something like that today?

Afterward, The Yardbirds packed up their gear and headed for Washington, DC, The Admirals played a final set, and it was over.

It was an amazing evening.

Kerb was on the air the whole time. About eleven-thirty I gave him a brief report. "We did good. See you in the morning."

The Divvy

On Saturdays, Kerby was on the air from 10 AM to 2PM. I did news from noon to 2, then records from 2 to 6.

Carrying a brown paper 'super-market' bag, I arrived at the station and went into the studio where Kerb was on the air. Inside the bag was his share of the previous evening's proceeds, mostly $1 bills wrapped in bundles of fifty.

I pulled up a chair behind Kerby. He started a record, then spun his chair around facing me. I began pulling bundles of bills from the bag and counting.

"One, two, three," I counted. "Eight, nine, ten. Fifteen, sixteen, seventeen. These last two small ones are fives and tens."

"My God, Paul, how much is this?"

"We each made one-thousand eighty-five dollars … you, Marty, and me."

At the time our salaries were $245 per-week. After tax and deductions our take-home was a bit over $200.

We'd earned the equivalent of five weeks net pay in one evening.

We looked at each other and said, "This is the most cash I've ever seen."

Stunning.

Check

The Yardbirds success convinced us that we should bring artists to Eudowood more often. Our next choice was Wilson Pickett.

A few months later we booked Pickett for a Friday night gig. Pickett cost $1,800.00. Nine-hundred dollars paid by check at signing of the contract, and the remainder due in cash between the first and second show.

Great crowd. Great performance.

(Nothing like the Yardbirds ... but hey ... they were free.) The three of us divided nearly $900.00

Fall, 1965.

Many of the kids asked us to bring Pickett back.

Marty was thinking maybe a Sunday afternoon appearance would work.

Nothing else happening, right?

Piece o'cake.

We booked Pickett for a Sunday in late October. Fee: $1,600.00 – $800 in front and $800 (cash) between shows.

Wilson Pickett was a real professional. He was always on time, his band always looked great, and he worked his tail off putting on great shows.

This Sunday was no different.

Well, actually it was different.

Again, Pickett was the ultimate entertainer.

Problem was, not enough people came to see him.

At show time, Pickett and his band hit the stage and worked it hard for the two-hundred or so in attendance.

Kerb and I were on the hook for $800 but were about $300 short.

Checkmate
"Wilson, we're about three-hundred dollars short of the eight hundred we owe you. So here's six-hundred and a check for the other three-hundred."

"No man. No checks."

Ulp!

"Aww, c'mon Wilson. The check is one-hundred percent good."

"What do the contract say?"

"It says cash."

"Right. I git the cash ... I'm on stage in a flash."

"But Wilson, we've booked you before."

"How'd I do?"

"You were great."

"Um hmm. How'd I do today?"

"Great."

"An' the second show gonna be jes' as good. Soon's I git my money."

Groveling now, I said, "You know we're a couple of top DJs in Baltimore and we play your records a lot."

"That's what yer s'posed to do, right?"

"Well … yeah."

"Right. Now git me the money so I can git on the stage an' do what I'm s'posed ta do."

"Geez Wilson, I thought we were friends."

Pickett looks me in the eye and says: "Lemme tell ya sumptin'. Friendship is friendship, but bidness is bidness."

Kerb and I left the dressing room and headed to the parking lot where over a hundred kids had congregated. We cajoled them into coming in.

That got us what we needed to give 'all cash' to Pickett.

Ever true to his word, Pickett took the stage and flat tore it up.

———

You might be wondering, "Why was the crowd so sparse?"

We certainly were.

Well ... the Baltimore Colts (the genuine Colts) were playing the Green Bay Packers at Memorial Stadium that Sunday afternoon.

Bad planning on our part?

Nope.

No planning.

Pickett Revisited

By mid-1966 Kerby had left WCAO for a TV show on Channel 11. He was about to become the Dick Clark of Baltimore.

I moved the dances to the Parkville National Guard Armory ...

... and re-booked Wilson Pickett.

I don't recall which local band played that evening, but if other bands weren't otherwise engaged it wasn't unusual for their members to attend our dances. On this particular evening that proved to be serendipitous.

———

We opened the doors around 7:45 PM. The band started at eight.

I went to the dressing room to see Pickett. He and most of his band were there.

Not his drummer.

Pickett was furious.

"I get my hands on that m^%*#@ I'mona kill him. He's pulled this s*!t for the las' time. He's fired."

I could go on.

Anyway, in a few minutes Pickett asked me if I knew if there was anyone here that could play drums.

Do I?

'Deed I do!

It so happened that Randy Pfeiffer was on the scene. He was the drummer for Denny and the Hitch-Hikers, a band that played all of Pickett's hits and did so very well.

I said, "Yeah, Wilson, there is."

"Git 'im."

I spotted Randy in the crowd.

"Hey Randy. Wanna play with Pickett tonight?"

Randy damn near jumped out of his skin.

"Ohm'GodYes!"

"Come with me."

I took Randy back to the dressing room and introduced him to Pickett, telling Wilson, "… this is the young man who can do the job for you tonight."

Pickett was skeptical. ("Really? A white high school kid can kick as well as my drummer? I don't think so.")

"So, ya say ya know all my songs?"

"Yes sir, Mr. Pickett."

"All of 'em?"

"All your hits, and some of the stuff on your albums."

"Right. OK, but lissen. I don' wan ya kicking no fancy s^#t back there, yaunnerstan'? No fancy s^#t! Just gimme that 'ficka blap, ficka blap, ficka blap. Got it?"

Yes sir, I got it."

"Les' go."

Randy absolutely blew Wilson Pickett away.

He played two sets and never missed a lick. I assumed he was having the time of his life.

I seem to recall that Pickett gave Randy $100.00. If he didn't he should have.

SIDEBAR: After he finished college Randy joined the media sales staff at WCBM where I was also employed. I haven't seen Randy since the fall of 1972 but I believe he still lives in the Baltimore area. Perhaps a reader can put us in touch.

CHAPTER TEN

DEVIL WITH A BLUE DRESS

Did I mention the unusually large number of outstanding bands we had in Baltimore?

There were many.

Comprised mainly of high school and college age white guys, these bands concentrated on 'covering' the songs of the great soul acts of the day because 'soul music' was what the white kids of Baltimore preferred. No ... demanded.

In order to be able to replicate the sound of these great records the bands needed trumpet, trombone and sax players and the good bands had them.

Again, these young musicians were talented, well-taught and very well-rehearsed. They took their music very seriously.

Had James Brown, Eddie Floyd, Otis Redding, Wilson Pickett, Sam and Dave, the Motown people, et al come to Baltimore and heard these kids playing their songs, they would have been astounded.

Yes. They really were that good.

(To me it was simple. Great training, great talent and lots of effort combined to make this happen, much like the factors resulting in the forming of 'Chicago' and the creation of their fabulous hit records. Re: Chicago? Having Peter Cetera as lead singer didn't hurt.)

The Word Is Out

One of the record promotion guys came to me one day.

He'd been told that I knew a lot about the local bands because I'd been hiring them for my 'record hops' every week.

"Are any of these guys any good?"

("Hmmm. Is he scouting around for talent for some of his labels?")

You bet they're good. Why do you ask?"

"Someone told Mitch Ryder about 'em."

(Whaaat?)

"Ryder wants his band to sound more like Pickett or James Brown. He's gonna add horns and a keyboard player and he's lookin' for young white guys to fill those slots. He said he wants to talk to you. OK?"

The next afternoon Mitch Ryder called.

"I heard you have great bands in Baltimore. True?"

"Yep."

"Tell me more."

"It's mostly college age white guys. Horn players, keyboardists, excellent drummers. All good musicians. No doubt about it. They take their music seriously."

"I want to come to Baltimore and hear these guys. Will you set up auditions for me?"

We set a date.

Goin' On The Road

I booked the Parkville Armory for a Saturday afternoon and invited several bands. I told them they'd be playing for Mitch Ryder and there was a chance they'd be asked to join the new Detroit Wheels.

Five bands came, including The Majestics and The Princetons.

Mitch Ryder? He came. He listened. He was blown away.

(This was sort of an 'I told you so,' but then I had an advantage: I'd been listening to these kids play week after week, some of them for three years or more. Yes indeed. They were mighty damn good.)

At the end of the day Mitch asked five of them to join him for rehearsals in New York.

Three musicians from The Majestics and two from the Princeton's said 'yes'.

From the Majestics: Frank Invernizzi (keyboard), Don Lehnhoff (trombone), and Jimmy Loomis (tenor sax). From the Princetons: Bob Shipley (saxophone) and Jimmy Wilson (trumpet).

Don Lehnhoff takes it from here.

Autumn of 1966

I don't remember who called me, but the Majestics (with me on trombone) were called by Baltimore DJ Paul Rodgers to play for Mitch Ryder. Mitch was following his management's big idea of going "blue-eyed-soul," leaving the Detroit Wheels rock band for a Wilson Pickett-style R&B band with horns, and he was looking for musicians in Baltimore based on the City's reputation for bands. In 1966 my plan was to finish Peabody Conservatory, then put the degree on the shelf for a while and play professionally. It was a good plan, but the professional opportunity arrived before the degree. Twenty years old and unfocused as a student, I couldn't turn it down.

[It should be noted that two other Majestics, Ray DeMoss on tenor and Duke Gore on bass, were originally offered those gigs and did turn them down – both in school and already knowing what they wanted their futures to be.]

On the bus from Baltimore to New York it was all anticipation and no clue. 1966 was a period of cultural fermentation, and much of that was taking place in New York. It was 2 years after the Beatles hit the US but 1 year before the Summer of Love, and 3 years before Woodstock. It was the year Andy Warhol introduced Lou Reed to Nico and produced the Velvet Underground's first album, with his art on the cover. Just being there with it happening all around us was exciting at the time, and historic in retrospect.

We arrived at the Port Authority bus terminal, and took up residence in the Coliseum Hotel on the Upper West Side for a month of rehearsal before hitting the road. Every day we rehearsed in a dance studio above the popular Cheetah night club, Broadway and 53rd, kitty-corner from the Ed Sullivan Theater. We ran charts written by a little old guy whose name I wish I remembered. Other tunes we did as head arrangements. We learned dance routines from choreographer Jaime Rogers, a dancer (Loco) in the Puerto Rican gang of "West Side Story," and choreographer for a lot of film and television. One top-10 memory was Jaime inviting me and my roommate, Jimmy Loomis, to jam for his improvisational dance class at the June Taylor Studios. I was banging on drums right there on the very wood floor where June and her girls worked out dance routines for the Jackie Gleason Show. That was cool.

Halfway through rehearsals we changed road managers, why I never exactly knew. The new RM was a British guy named Brian Condliffe, recent road manager for the Yardbirds and Jeff Beck's 'best friend' he said. His presence at this time, when British music was exploding in America, really rounded out the cultural universe for us; and Brian was a good guy to boot.

Living in NYC, 1967
I sat in Ondine's, a small club on East 59th Street, and listened to the house band – the Doors. They were just starting to make a reputation. I sat in the same club listening to Buffalo Springfield. Stephen Stills and Neil Young weren't yet names, any more than drummer Dewey Martin or guitar/singer Richie Furay. They were just part of a band. On break, Stills came to our table to talk to Mitch.

We also went to The Scene, a club in the basement of 301 West 46th Street in New York's Theater District, owned by Steve Paul. Paul was a musical impresario of sorts and I saw Tiny Tim there, also the Velvet Underground and the Youngbloods.

After a month, rehearsals wrapped and we hit the road. Life on the road is a whole other story, and after our first 3 months of touring we were back in home base New York to do the Murray the K Easter Show – 28 shows in 9 days. Mitch Ryder had top billing with Wilson Pickett. Making their first appearance in the U.S., a couple of British bands just getting started – The Who and Cream — were further down the bill. The Who were so committed to their "destroy-the-instruments" routine that they even smashed their drums and guitars in rehearsal. True professionals. After each performance their roadie would pile it all on a dolly and wheel it backstage to a workshop he set up in a tiny backstage room. There he bolted, glued and screwed things back together for the next show. After the final show it all just went into a dumpster.

Sometimes you got out for some air between shows and sometimes you just hung out, or napped, in the dressing room. I remember socializing backstage with the great Canadian band, Mandala, and with Wilson Pickett's super drummer at that time – Buddy Miles. I also remember Wilson Pickett's "valet" touring the dressing rooms with two professional ladies in tow, Tiger Baby and her sister whose name escapes me.

After the last show there was a wrap party of sorts – a jam session at The Scene. The Scene was squarely in Andy Warhol's sphere, with his celebrity screen prints on the wall, his band the Velvet Underground on stage, and his personal presence on the dance floor cavorting with a movie camera. That jam night Ginger Baker and Jack Bruce backed up Buddy Miles singing the blues. Eric Clapton was there, too cool to jam, sitting at a table getting drunk.

We went back on the road, and after almost 7 months with Mitch my "Greetings" letter from Uncle Sam finally arrived; my safety valve against a life of rock and roll debauchery had been activated. I knew it would be coming sooner or later after quitting college in the pre-lottery draft era. Seven months was probably about right.

Through this whole adventure I met the great Mike Bloomfield. I also met a guy from Spanky and Our Gang, a guy from the New Christie Minstrels, Question Mark & the Mysterions ('96 Tears'), Art Linkletter, a fraternity at the University of Indiana (where I became a 'Cardinal') ... and the woman I would marry forever, 18 months later. It must have been destiny.

In retrospect, Mitch owed me one. I should have asked him to play a free concert for me.

Otis And The Temps

At the same time Mitch Ryder was in town, Otis Redding and The Temptations were headlining a show at the Baltimore Civic Center. Mitch wanted to attend.

"Get a couple tickets. Way in the back. I don't want anyone to know I'm there."

Mitch and I sat in the 'way-back.' 'Little' Stevie Wonder opened the show.

Otis and The Temps were fabulous. (I envied Melvin Franklin, the Temptations bass singer. I wanted his job!)

In my opinion Otis Redding was the greatest 'blues singer' of the era. Not even a contest. Want proof? Listen to Otis sing "My Lover's Prayer," "These Arms of Mine," "I've Been Loving You Too Long," or "Pain In My Heart."

No one could beg like Otis. He was my favorite by a mile.

Note: At age twenty-six Otis Redding was killed in a plane crash, in December of 1967. The Day The Music Died II.

G Goodman

Speaking of the record promoters ...

This group of ten or twelve guys began each week facing a near-impossible task: getting their records on the playlists of the top radio stations.

Most stations added from three to seven 'new' titles in a given week but collectively, in that same week, the promotion men would have as many as 100 new records to promote.

New releases by top hit artists always got priority, making it a near impossibility to convince a PD to take a chance on a new artist.

Fact: Top-rated stations in big markets rarely 'broke' new artists.

They played the hits, but they didn't make the hits. That was left to stations in the small markets that could more easily take a chance on playing a new release, because they were less concerned with ratings than their big city brethren.

When a record by a new artist started racking up sales in the smaller markets … in other words, 'proving itself' … the record companies would get behind it, and the promotion men would have a story to tell to the PD's of the bigger stations.

That's how new artists got their records on the playlists of big-market stations.

With 50 to 100 new releases each week, you can imagine the number of records that went unplayed, and thus unheard, both by PDs and by the general public. The promotion men had a tough row to hoe.

Baltimore was blessed with many good promotion men. Joe Bilello, Bernie Block, Joe Cash, Ed DeJoy, Bill Jamison, Earl Rollison, Fred Tevis, Bill Turner and Zim Zemarel, to name a few.

Each week these guys would battle the PDs, hoping to garner one (or more) of the 'new adds' to the following weeks play list. Amazingly, these guys were virtually unflappable.

George Goodman was the coolest I ever met.

'Georgie' was a tall, handsome African-American man who (as I recall) hailed from Pittsburgh. We were about the same age.

Like me, George was a fan of doo-wop music. I recall him telling me that he used to sing in a group that actually made some recordings. He worked for Schwartz Brothers, a large distributor based in Washington, DC.

George was always dressed to the nines – understated but elegant. Had there been an annual award for 'best-dressed promo man' George would have retired the trophy.

And he had a way with words.

As a DJ, I had nothing at all to do with what records were added to the playlist. I did have some discretion re how often they got played. Meaning that it was now and then productive for the promo men to ask me to 'give them a little help' with a record.

In other words, 'when you have a choice in the matter it would be cool if you'd give me an extra spin or two of the new [insert artist here] record'.

As 'payment' for such favors we occasionally received promo copies of albums to use as prizes at our record hops and other appearances.

(I started on the air in June of 1958. Shortly thereafter the payola scandal broke wide open. These albums – and an Irish Rovers commemorative cup – are the closest I ever came to payola of any kind. The Payola scandal was responsible for many stories, none of which include my name. Thankfully.)

One afternoon George was in the DJ 'break room' talking with me about a new release from Neil Diamond. He asked if I'd give it a few extra spins.

I was a Neil Diamond fan.

"No problem."

For a minute or two we talked about Diamond's superb song-writing talent and the fact that many of his lyrics were quite touching.

Georgie: "Umm hmm. The man can turn a phrase."

Biscuits

A few minutes later George made for the door, heading to another radio station.

"See ya later Georgie."

Stopping at the doorway George turned.

With a smile he coolly raised his index finger, pointed it at me and said,

"Yeah man. Spin them biscuits."

George Goodman always handled his business with purpose and professionalism. He was a great guy, one of the coolest cats I ever met.

As I recall, George Goodman died in an in-home accident in 1968.

CHAPTER ELEVEN

MOVIN' ON

In radio broadcasting terms the 1960s should be described as "JBFM" – Just Before FM.

AM stations dominated the ratings because they'd 'gotten there first' with the most desired programming. Yes, FM stations were on the air but very few had listening audiences of any size.

Most FM licenses had been picked up by companies with AM stations, primarily to lay claim to the spectrum space 'in case anything good ever happens'.

For programming, the AM broadcasters simply chose to 'hot-house' the FM by simulcasting their AM format.

Unimaginative, but cheap.

Spectrum space controlled? Check. FM station running at near-zero cost? Check. No changes on the horizon so we'll continue to work our AM – it's the money maker? Check.

With little to no consumer demand in the offing, manufacturers were uninterested in making and/or promoting the sale of FM receivers.

———

Baltimore radio of the 1960s featured over twenty AM and/or FM stations on the air in the metro. Only five stations mattered. All were AMs.

WBAL – A Hearst Corporation 50kw 'flamethrower' at 1090 on the dial. Sister station to NBC TV affiliate, Channel 11 and the Baltimore News-American newspaper.

WBAL featured local personalities, news, Oriole baseball and Baltimore Colt football. (The authentic Colts – accept no Indianapolis substitutes).

Musically they were in an MOR (middle-of-the-road) format featuring Frank Sinatra, Tony Bennett, Eydie Gorme, Vic Damone, Dean Martin, etc.

At night WBAL featured The Harley Show. More on that coming up.

WFBR – Locally owned 5kw semi-clone of WBAL at 1300, also playing MOR music but with a much smaller footprint and no sports franchises.

WWIN – Also locally owned, and the best of the three stations programmed to reach Baltimore's large African-American community.

With 500 watts at 1400 on the dial, WWIN featured some of Baltimore's best radio personalities. People like Maurice 'Hot Rod' Hulbert: "Hey Big Mommy-O, Big Poppy-O and Keen Teen. You got the Nahhd from the Rahhhhd! The man with no hair and no worldly care. Stand by for the blast off ..."

Hot Rod - July, 1966
https://youtu.be/PCRwqiBGDEw

And Paul 'Fat Daddy' Johnson. "Here's a Fat Poppa Show Stoppah baby. The Temmm – Tashionzzzz Tationzzz."

Fat Daddy - Summer, 1966
https://youtu.be/24Z46qQV34o

WCBM – Owned by Metro Media and broadcast with 10kw at 680 on the dial, the station featured top local personalities, played MOR music, and featured a ten-person full-time news staff that provided the best local/regional news coverage in the market.

WCBM was sister station to top-rated WNEW New York, WIP Philadelphia, KNEW San Francisco, WLAC Los Angeles, and other great radio stations in large metros across the US.

WCAO – Owned by Plough, Inc., manufacturers of OTC pharmaceutical products such as St. Joseph's Aspirin for Children, Coppertone Suntan Lotion, etc.

WCAO broadcast with 5kw at 600 on the AM dial. Plough also owned stations in four other markets. The Plough stations were 'early adopters' of the Top 40 format and all, at one time or another, were rated number one in their markets.

The Harley Show

No review of Baltimore radio of the 1950s and '60s would be deemed complete without at least a mention of perhaps the most unique radio show of that, or perhaps any era.

At 11:30 each night listeners in Baltimore, and DXers from northernmost Canada to the southernmost tip of Florida, from the Mississippi River to waaay out in the Atlantic Ocean, tuned their radios to 1090 AM where they heard "Things Ain't What They Used To Be," a Duke Ellington tune featuring Johnny Hodges on tenor sax, open 'The Harley Show'.

Dig it here:

"Things Ain't What They Used To Be"
https://youtu.be/yzPgYo19AsQ

This all jazz music show was hosted by Harley Brinsfield who boasted the largest collection of jazz records in the world, and backed his claim with encyclopedic knowledge of the musicians, the composers, the tunes, where they were recorded, when the record was released, etc., and talked about it every weeknight.

This was a rolling history lesson in the evolution of American jazz music and how it influenced many other genres of American music.

The show ran from 11:30 PM to 1:00 AM and was sponsored by Harley's Sandwich Shops, owned by – you guessed it – Harley Brinsfield. Harley had shops all over Baltimore and throughout Maryland, which at the time made him the proprietor of one of America's first and largest fast food franchises, pre-dating McDonald's. He made a helluva sandwich!

———

"Lightly Lightly, Once Over Nightly, and Ever so Politely, This is The Harley Show. Music Outta Baltimore. Radio Like Radio Used To Sound."

This was Harley's show opener, just before he launched into the music of that evening's Featured Artist. One of those in particular caught my ear, the great Clyde McCoy.

Treat yourself by checking out some o' these licks.

"Sugar Blues"
https://youtu.be/SjemjB3kgAM

The Harley Show always ended with Bob Scobey's Frisco Jazz Band's recording of 'Sailin' Down Chesapeake Bay' … vocal by Clancy Hayes. Appropriate, no?

Give it a listen! And while you're at it, why not sing along.

"Sailin' Down Chesapeake Bay"
https://www.youtube.com/watch?v=z99FxoowHPA

Come on, Nancy, put your best dress on.
Come on, Nancy, 'fore the steamboat's gone.
Everything is lovely on the Chesapeake Bay,
All aboard for Baltimore, and if we're late they'll all be sore!
Now look here, Captain, let us catch that boat.
We can't swim, and listen, we can't float!
Banjo's strumming a good old tune,
Up on deck is the place to spoon.
Cuddle up close beneath the silv'ry moon,
Sailin' down the Chesapeake Bay.

—Words by Jean C. Havez, Music by George Botsford.

FYI, lyricist Mr. Havez was born in Baltimore in 1869 and graduated from Johns Hopkins University in 1893. Composer, Mr. Botsford, was born in Sioux Falls, SD in 1874 and spent most of his career in New York City.

The Big Time
Every night from May through November, as I left the station for home, I tuned to 1090 AM and listened to Harley.

Every single night. I can still hear it in my mind's ear.

I was mesmerized by the variety of outstanding programming on the various big-time radio stations in Baltimore and nearby Washington DC, and particularly so with Mr. Brinsfield, his knowledge and his unique on-air style.

The Harley Show was confirmation that I had arrived in, and was now a part of, certified Big Time Radio. Wow, did that ever make me feel good.

True, I loved 'our' music. But I also loved Harley's music and The Harley Show.

I love it to this very day.

Ratings

WCAO consistently led in the ratings starting in the late fifties, nearly always garnering at least a 35 share of the 12+ audience, often topping 40 shares with adults 18-34, and 30 shares with adults 18-44.

WBAL claimed a 20 share of the 12+ audience and often had a 30 share of those listeners over age 49.

WCBM had a 12 share of the 12+ audience, their core audience being in the 25-54 age demographic.

WWIN also claimed a 10 share, their audience being comprised primarily of African-Americans.

WFBR had an 8 share of the audience, made up of those listeners who liked them better than they liked WBAL or WCBM.

The other stations vied for the remaining meager pickings.

Shot In The Foot

In Baltimore, the last 'format war' of any significance occurred in 1960.

WCAO was wounded. It was a self-inflicted wound.

In an apparent attempt at self-immolation, WCAO shattered the 'if it ain't broke, don't fix it' rule by turning away from the pure Top Forty format that had them ruling the roost with a 40 share of the audience.

How could this happen?

Here's what I was told. This, directly from 'The Land of Make Believe'.

In love with what they perceived as the superior-to-man brain power of the computer (at that time a sensational new device), the Plough Corporate Program Director decided that given the right information, a computer could design the perfect music list, insuring that the station would always – always – be playing a song that 100% of the available listening audience would absolutely love, thus guaranteeing never-before-achieved mega shares of the listening audience.

(What? A 40-share wasn't enough?)

Using the top hit records of the preceding five to ten years, they fed the song titles, lyrics, tune patterns and tempos, instrumentation, male/female/group voices, song keys, record sales figures, chart positions, and on and on ... into a computer. Any piece of information that could ever have been deemed a factor in a record being loved by the public was (somehow) reduced to data and entered.

Next, they asked the computer to spit out the perfect library of available songs, and also design the play list to use on-air.

(Remember: This was 1960-61 when rock and roll tunes were taking over dominance of the pop music charts.)

The computer coughed out a mish-mosh rotation of tunes that made no sense.

Tony Bennett followed by The Miracles followed by Patsy Cline followed by a big band tune followed by Fats Domino followed by Peggy Lee followed by the Mitch Miller Orchestra followed by James Brown.

Play and repeat.

Plough's belief in the deductive power of the computer was so thorough that they took this information as infallible and implemented the music format in all of their markets.

Listeners left the stations in droves.

Five (mostly) #1 rated stations were trashed.

Pipsqueak Wins ... Temporarily
In Baltimore, Jake Embry's WITH (a 250 watt pop gun) immediately jumped in with a pure Top 40 format and snatched ten to fifteen shares from WCAO. Their tiny footprint is all that prevented the damage from being far worse.

———

But wait!

In Baltimore, WCAO General Manager Bernie Millenson saw what was happening and made an executive decision.

After just a month or two of the 'nonsense format' (and without notifying the home office) he took the station back to its previous music formatting. Almost immediately the audience began to return.

Footnote: WCAO permanently lost ten audience shares to WITH and other stations and never again posted 35 shares in the ratings. In spite of that, WCAO still dominated the primary Adult 18-49 demographic and was the 'cash cow' for Plough Broadcasting for another fifteen years.

The other Plough stations never recovered.

Hot AC

In 1968 on the West Coast, a creative program director named Joe Kelley developed an offshoot of the Top Forty format, a 'new format' called Hot Adult Contemporary, or 'Hot AC'. Aimed squarely at the 25-44 age demographic, Hot AC featured 'non-rock' present day hits neatly mixed with a delicious array of the great oldies from the fifties/early sixties.

'No rock' made the format unattractive to teens (great for ad sales), and the rock 'n' roll hits of the fifties and early sixties had never been embraced by folks now over fifty, but for everyone between 25 and 49 – known in advertising circles as The Money Demographic – the Hot AC format was dead solid perfect!

In any given hour a Hot AC station listener could enjoy a Dionne Warwick hit song, something from Elton John, an Elvis oldie, a Sergio Mendes - Brazil '66 tune, something groovy from the Temptations (My Girl?), Frank Sinatra's 'It Was A Very Good Year' and a Billy Joel hit. To this add 50s songs by the Platters or Rick Nelson, sprinkled amongst great songs by the Bee Gees, Bread and The Beatles, and you had the perfect mix.

Hot AC also required top radio personalities, great station jingles, lots of out-of-station listener contact and fun contests.

The format took off like a rocket in market after market, soaring to the top of the ratings in the 25-49 age demographic, and stealing listeners from Top Forty stations playing loud rock music, and from the MOR stations that sounded 'tired'.

In the fall of 1968, Joe Kelley was hired by Metro Media to come to Baltimore and change the format of WCBM from MOR to Hot AC.

WCBM joined the rocket ride.

Dan Donovan

Upon his arrival, one of Kelley's first hires was Dan Donovan, who joined the staff at WCBM doing Afternoon Drive.

I met DD when he was Blaine Harvey (his given name). In 1960 Blaine was hired to fill the slots at WSBA when the full-timers were on vacation. I was asked to get him acclimated to the workings of the console and our format.

Blaine was a full-time student at Penn State who wanted a career in broadcasting. We were kindred souls. We became the best of friends.

After graduation, Blaine joined Susquehanna Broadcasting at their station in Providence, RI, after which he went to work in Boston using the name Dan Donovan.

He became one of the top radio personalities in that market.

Then he showed up in Baltimore where we were head-to-head competitors, me on WCAO and Dan on WCBM, each of us striving to 'win' Baltimore's PM Drive Ratings Race. (More on that later.)

Night Clubbin'

The Club Venus opened in Baltimore in 1966. Seating for up to 500. A great spot for supper, drinks and top-class entertainment.

Imagine a star-studded rotation of acts like The Four Freshmen, Marvin Gaye, Sergio Franchi, Mel Tormé, Timi Yuro, and The Temptations. Even comedians such as Jackie Vernon, Sid Caesar and Jack E. Leonard.

And the shows were always backed by some of Baltimore's top bands, like The Admirals and Tommy Vann and the Echoes.

THE place to be!

Late in 1968, Capitol Records gave a party for Baltimore radio personalities celebrating the appearance of The Lettermen, a most successful act on their label.

I was doing Afternoon Drive on WCAO. Barbie and I were invited.

Capitol Promotion Men Bill Jamison and Bill Turner were hosting. Personalities from several of the stations attended.

We sat at a long, rectangular table, center-front and close to the stage. I sat next to Bill Jamison. He introduced me to the guy sitting across from me.

Joe Kelly.

————

Right to the Point.

Bill: "Paul, meet Joe Kelly, the new PD at WCBM. Joe, this is Paul Rodgers."

Me: "Nice to meet you, Joe."

Joe: "Nice to meet you, too. Hey, when are you going to go to work for a good radio station?"

Me: "As soon as a good radio station offers me a job."

Joe: "We'll have to see about that."

End of conversation.

————

The Lettermen were great.

They came to our table and sang "When I Fall In Love" to Barbie. It was her favorite song. She's never forgotten the moment.

I had nothing to do with it – they just picked her out of the group.

The Lettermen showed that they had excellent taste.

Pittsburgh Calling

A month or two later I got a call from the PD of a Pittsburgh radio station.

"Hey Paul. Got your audition tape and really like it. How about coming to work with us in Pittsburgh."

(Tape? What tape? I never sent a tape.)

"A tape? From me?"

"Yeah. Got it the other day. So what's it going to take to get you to Pittsburgh?"

I was earning $250/week at WCAO, and another $100 or so via record hops and personal appearances. More importantly, after a long time trying I'd just made my way into the field of free-lance commercial recording, which had the look of something that could be very good for me.

We loved Baltimore and Maryland, and our little country house. Our children were happy.

And I hadn't been looking.

"I dunno. A three year no-cut contract and about $500/week?"

"Wow! You must really like Baltimore."

"I do, but that's not the problem. I've been here five years. I'm kind of in demand for personal appearances and such, and I just made inroads into freelance commercial recording."

"You can do that in Pittsburgh, as well."

"Maybe, but after how long? I'm flattered and I thank you for your interest, but I believe it's best for me and my family if I stay where I am."

Truth?

Flattered doesn't even touch it – I felt great.

What triggered that call? I had no clue.

I hadn't sent anyone a tape.

What the heck just happened?

This would happen twice over the next eight or ten weeks. Calls from PDs at top stations in Detroit and St. Louis, trying to hire me.

I asked the Detroit PD where he got the tape.

"Joe Kelly sent it to me."

Bingo!

Kelley was sending audition tapes of me to other PDs. He wanted me out of Baltimore and out of Dan Donovan's hair.

Note: At the expense of sounding self-serving I must point out the following: As hard as they tried, WCBM was unable to move the Afternoon Drive needle away from WCAO. Their PM Drive ratings did increase, but the increase came at the expense of the other MOR stations. WCAO continued to 'rule the roost'.

Fifth Time's the Charm

"Hey Paul, it's Joe Kelley. Can you to meet me at my office after you get off the air – say around 7:30?"

"OK, sure."

"We're at 2610 N. Charles Street. See you then."

Joe met me at the door and we went upstairs to his office.

"You wanna hear a great record?"

It was March of 1969. Simon and Garfunkel's "The Boxer" enveloped the room. One of the all time great recordings.

———

"I need to get you outta there and I guess the only way to do that is to hire you," Kelly said. "Donovan's gonna leave soon. When he does I want you to be his replacement. You'll have to do evenings for a while, then it's back to PM Drive. Whaddya say? How does $350 sound?"

(Metro Media always appreciated air personalities and treated them accordingly. I saw this as a magnificent opportunity, one I could accept without leaving Baltimore. I couldn't say no. I didn't.)

"Sounds good to me."

"Great. How soon can you be here?"

Silent Praise

Well-known fact: In the broadcasting industry, when a radio personality resigns he's always, always paid off immediately – and shown the door.

Mantra: "If he's gone in his mind he needs to be outta here. No telling what he'd say if we left him on the air."

(But when he's 'going across the street' to a serious competitor? Whoa! Get him out the door yesterday!)

Think of it like a mega-contentious divorce ... on steroids.

This was April. The rating period had three weeks to go. Next day I went to my PD and resigned.

PD: "Where are you going?"

Me: "I'm going to WCBM." (I am so getting thrown outta here.)

PD: (long pause) – "Can you give me three weeks ... until the end of the rating period?"

I was absolutely floored.

I worked a three-week notice without incident.

I'd never heard of such a thing. Still haven't. And no one from WCAO management ever mentioned a word about this to me.

In retrospect, one of the finest compliments I ever received.

Whoops

A day or two after accepting the job at WCBM, Joe Kelly was called to Los Angeles. AFTRA was on strike in LA so Metro Media rounded up some 'used-to-be-on-the-air' management types and sent them to LA to work at KLRA until the strike was settled.

The word was out. Paul Rodgers was leaving WCAO for WCBM. A week or so after my resignation, Promotion Man Joe Bilello stopped me in the hall.

"Paul, I guess you heard – Joe Kelly was fired."

Me: (ulp!) – "Oh … mmm … yehhhh, I heard that (liar!) How'd it happen?"

"He was PO'ed that he had to work the overnight show and got mouthy with a Metro Media exec."

(Great! I'm hired at a new job that I haven't started. I've resigned my present job. The guy that hired me is gone and I'm going to work for someone I've never met? Now what?)

The next day I screwed up my courage and went to WCBM to see General Manager Don Kelley.

I expressed my alarm at the situation.

"Relax. We're happy that you decided to join us. Can't wait."

I worked for Don Kelley for three years. He was a terrific General Manager.

And new PD, Dale Andrews, was also excellent.

The next four years turned out to be the best of my seventeen years on the air.

Fixer Upper

There was a second move in the offing. This one involved the purchase, restoration, and occupancy of an old farmhouse in Baltimore County, thirty miles north of the city. Complete with barn and thirty-five acres of ground, the country place we'd always wanted.

The kids got a pony, Barbie redecorated (as only she can), and I got a flock of chickens, a tomato garden, and stuff to do on weekends.

Life was as good as it could possibly be.

CHAPTER TWELVE

SIMPLY THE BEST

Professionally speaking, I'd found nirvana.

Within a year of the format change to Hot AC, WCBM was rated Number One in the all-important Adults 25-44 audience demographic. Here's why.

Metromedia loved its radio stations and treated its employees with respect – including the air talent, where in many companies we were viewed as a 'necessary evil'.

At Metromedia we were valued teammates.

For me, doing afternoons on WCBM was a privilege, a pleasure and a blessing.

I was twenty-nine years old and an eleven year broadcast veteran. I still couldn't believe I was being paid to play records and say funny stuff.

Can you say, "Living the dream?"

The WCBM Staff

<u>Personalities</u>

Lee Case and Joe Knight teamed up to do mornings – 6 to 10 AM. Lee was the communicator. Joe the comedian. Both were highly intelligent and very talented. Between them they knew everyone (and every street) in Baltimore.

Both are Baltimore Radio Legends.

Dennis Murray (he of the big voice) was on from 10 AM to 2 PM. I did Afternoon Drive – 2 to 6 PM. Chuck Boyles followed me with two hours of telephone talk, 6 to 8 PM. (Note: Boyles was the successor to John Sterling, now the radio voice of the New York Yankees.)

Bob Galen was on the air from 8 to midnight. Ron Nabors did overnights.

They called us "The Entertain Men."

News Department

Bob 'Smoke' Shilling was WCBM's Award-Winning News Director. His large staff included Robert Burns, John Hartge (make note of that name), Dave Humphrey, Pat Nason, Bob Schmidt and Richard Sher.

'Dean' of the news staff was Eddie Fenton, whose twenty-five years on-air in Baltimore included two decades of political reporting. Fenton knew everyone in Baltimore and Annapolis.

And he knew where the bodies were buried – all of them.

Note: In any history of Baltimore radio performers, if you looked up the words 'irascible character' Fenton's picture would be there. His unbridled use of words like @%er, ##$t, and @#&#~le, was legendary!

No viable news story ever escaped the detection of this talented group. They were the best.

Sports

Charley Eckman, sports personality and legend extraordinaire, and Neal Eskridge, baseball writer for the News-American, each shared their unique perspective on sports. At one time or another in his career Eckman was an NBA and NCAA basketball referee, an NBA coach, a sportscaster, and maybe the funniest man ever to make a living in sports. And he adored Thoroughbred racing.

Special Features
Elane Stein's acerbic wit added a cynical reality to the daily proceedings.

Contests and Promotion
Headed by Promotions Director Joe Clarke, WCBM offered fun contests like Think Mink and the Truck-A-Luck, lots of on-location broadcasts, and plenty of print and TV advertising promoting the station, our news presence, and our community involvement.

THINK MINK: On the air we gave away certificates for mink stoles and coats. Then we took three or four busloads of listeners (with significant others) to Zinman Furs in Cherry Hill, New Jersey for a weekend bash, where our contest winners selected and 'modeled' the item of their choice. Top Class. Yes Indeed!

TRUCK-A-LUCK: Loaded with many hundreds of dollars in prizes, the WCBM van would pull up and park in front of a randomly-selected house. "The WCBM van is parked in front of 995 First Street in

Catonsville. If you live at 995 First Street in Catonsville you have 68 seconds to come out and claim all the prizes in the van. Paul Rodgers is there to greet you."

Music

Ahh, the music. Our Hot AC format was a blend of the best of the current (non-rock) hits, with the great oldies of the fifties and sixties, including album cuts – truly a one-of-a-kind music rotation for Baltimore radio.

WCBM was the first Hot AC station east of the Mississippi.

WCBM was a smash hit in Baltimore.

The Paul Rodgers Radio Program
I was the PM Drive personality, on-air from 2 to 6 PM. I'm an afternoon-evening person so my life clock made 'takin' 'em home from work' the perfect fit.

And did we ever have fun.

I loved the music. I loved (and love) Baltimore and Baltimoreans. I relished the two-way communication with these wonderful people who honored me by listening and responding to the nuttiness.

I made my living with lots of local presence and knowledge, outrageous puns, and the ability to tell the time in dozens. Example: Ten after three was 'two under a dozen past half a half dozen'. I did this six or seven times each week. It drove listeners crazy.

Both of them!

———

The Henry J was a 1950s automobile built by the Kaiser-Frazer Corporation and named after its chairman, Henry J. Kaiser. Production started in 1950 and ended in 1954.

Mr. Kaiser wanted to offer a car that could be built inexpensively and thus be affordable (approx. $1,300.00) for the average American. This was an early attempt to brand and market an American compact car.

The cost was kept down because the car offered so few components. Example: No rear trunk lid (owners accessed the trunk by folding down the rear seat). Initially the car was offered only as a 2-door sedan with fixed rear windows. It had no armrests, no glove compartment, no passenger-side sun visor and no flow- through ventilation.

(By now you can understand why this car failed to last!)

OK. So ... it's March 16, 1972 around 12:45 PM.

I'm driving down the Jones Falls Expressway en route to the station, and I pass ... a Henry J. All shiny and looking brand new, it was.

I hadn't seen one of these for almost twenty years. In my mind's ear I heard the jingle they once used for their radio and TV ads.

"The Henry J. The Henry J. America's Cheering the Henry J."

I couldn't get it out of my mind.

On my show that afternoon I talked about the car and 'treated' the audience to my rendition of the jingle.

A few days later this postcard arrived in the mail:

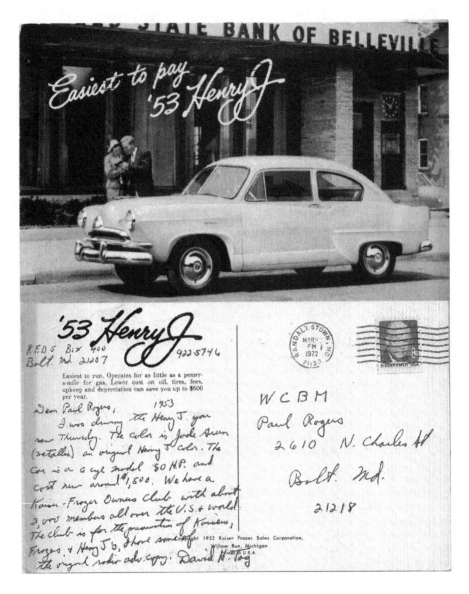

You never know who might be listening.

Hello Rodgerzzzz

That's Charley Eckman, greeting me whilst returning from the race track. Charley (and his cigar) did five minutes of sports at 4:35 and 5:35, often ending stories with "... and if you don't believe that, you can call a cab." (If he really wanted to make the point he'd add, "And if you still don't believe it you can call two cabs!")

Baltimore loved Charley because he said what was on his mind.

If I may. If you're a sports fan, or if you simply enjoy reading about real American characters, I highly recommend "It's A Very Simple Game – The Life and Times of Charley Eckman," written by Eckman and Fred Neil. Trust me. You don't have to be from Baltimore to enjoy this one.

Tsk

Elane Stein was a highly opinionated, very sophisticated lady who joined me three afternoons each week for a five minute feature on ... well, "... whatever I damn well choose."

Elane once did four hilarious minutes on Brussels Sprouts.

(Brussels Sprouts? Funny? Who coulda guessed?)

Trust me.

I wish I had a recording.

Elane was to WCBM as Andy Rooney was to 60 Minutes.

This wonderful lady passed away on October 1, 2008.

**WCBM/680
ELANE STEIN**

Payback Is Hell

Dave Humphrey was the PM Drive news guy – 'My Newsman'. No one ever did it better. Best of all our personalities clicked, making for some very interesting repartee.

After each 'cast Dave and I would kick something around for a few seconds before getting back to the music, etc.

Dave had a tendency to talk himself into a corner, after which I'd give him a wise guy one-liner (while turning off his mike), then hit the jingle and start a record.

He had no time to deliver a comeback.

I'd been getting the best of Dave for a very long time.

On Monday afternoon, November 8, 1971, Dave paid me back.

I mean he really paid me back. Big time.

Playing a Monday Night Football game in Baltimore, the Colts hosted a noon luncheon for the press. Dave attended along with the ABC TV broadcast team – Frank Gifford, Don Meredith and Howard Cosell.

After lunch, Dave cornered Howard Cosell and told him how I'd been zinging him. Then he asked if Cosell would deliver a couple of insulting comments about "Paul Rodgers."

Cosell agreed. Dave recorded two.

That afternoon, right after the 4:30 news, I opened the mike to talk with Dave. I spoke for two or three seconds when Dave hit me with a Humphrey/Cosell Nuclear Strike.

Howard Cosell slams Paul
http://emperorrodgers.com/Chap12-1.mp3

I was dumbstruck – dead in the water. For the first time in my career I had no rejoinder.

I fumbled, stumbled, mumbled something stupid and played a record.

I turned around to see Humphrey doubled up with laughter.

————

Round Two.

After the 5:30 news Dave hit me again.

Cosell kicks Paul while he's down
http://emperorrodgers.com/Chap12-2.mp3

Nobody did a more authoritative put-down than Howard Cosell. Those two 'shots' made the score between me and Dave even-steven.

SIDEBAR: Many stations were implementing formats that tightened personalities and restricted content. At WCBM we were encouraged to 'go with the flow of the day'. We played lots of music, but always mixed in on-air interaction with listeners and colleagues.

I have no recordings of the proceedings, and it's impossible to convey the joy that I experienced and the privilege I felt to be a member of this staff of talented radio people.

Ratings were through the roof. We must have been doing something right.

Arnold George Dorsey

Al Saunders Lesson One: 'Ya gotta know what they are thinking about."

Englebert Humperdinck was a big star – big voice, big ballads, big arrangements.

Not so big with the soul music/rock 'n' roll crowd. Square, even.

For women in the 25-54 age demographic – prime audience for us – he was adored.

EH records were a perfect accoutrement to our more up-tempo format. From Les Bicyclettes de Belsize to Winter World of Love, I played one nearly every afternoon.

Somebody noticed. Actually, a lot of very important somebodies.

A lady called one afternoon, gushing about how much she loved Englebert Humperdinck and how pleased she was that I played his records, because, "… you're the only DJ in Baltimore that ever plays his songs, and I love him, and all my friends love him, and … and … thank you sooo much."

"No problem, Ma'am. He's a star because he makes great records."

"Ohhh, I'm so happy that you like him. Please, please keep playing his songs."

Thus began a string of conversations that lasted for the rest of my time at WCBM.

Our conversations grew in length, then quickly broadened to include many of "… all my friends," and before I knew it I'd been dubbed Baltimore's Official Englebert Humperdinck DJ.

Barbie and I were invited to (and attended) several EHFC meetings in various member's homes, meetings attended by EH fans who had become avid WCBM listeners. Great folks enjoying the music they loved. What could be better?

It was easy for me to engage listeners in conversation, 'reaching out' if you will.

When I did that they reached back – in spades.

These wonderful people of Baltimore were treating me like I 'was somebody'. In reality, it was I who should have been doing the treating.

I was honored that they decided to join me on the radio, and that they told their friends about WCBM and the great music we played.

While this was definitely not as 'cool' as being the OBDJ (Official Beatles Disc Jockey), for WCBM and me it was a perfect building block in us becoming a bigger part of the lives of Baltimore's adult radio listeners and the community.

And while I liked the Beatles and much of their music – we played a bunch of it – I was truly 'over' any need to appeal to teenyboppers.

Sadly, I can't remember the name of the lady whose phone call started this. She knows who she is.

Thank you, Ma'am.

BTW: Englebert Humperdinck's real name is Arnold George "Gerry" Dorsey. The original 'EH' was a 19th century German composer of operas.

No Fair At The Fair
WCBM was the Official Radio Station of the Maryland State Fair, held each September at the fairgrounds in Timonium, a northern suburb of Baltimore.

Every day we broadcast live from the fairgrounds, giving us the opportunity to meet lots of our listeners face to face.

Fair promoters thought it a great idea for us to stage a cow milking contest in the area of the dairy barn.

Having no thoughts whatsoever of participating himself, our PD quickly agreed. I was tabbed to 'compete' in this contest vs. our 'All Night Satellite,' Ron Nabors.

For the next week or so Ron and I kicked this around on our shows, promoting the day, time and location for the contest and inviting listeners to come and observe the festivities.

Ron went on and on about how he was going to 'out milk' me, and the rest of the DJs chimed in with their thoughts on the matter.

Several hundred folks were in attendance as two champion Holstein dairy cows (they're the black and white ones) were led into the arena to meet us.

The ref explained the rules: "You have sixty seconds to get milk into your bucket. The guy with the most milk wins. No cross-squirting allowed."

We each took a bucket and went to our assigned cow.

Nabors approached 'Betty' with fear and trepidation.

Other than "I guess ya' gotta pull on these," he had no idea how to get milk from a cow.

"What? No spigot? Do I crank the tail? Whaaat! Helllp!"

I pulled my stool up to 'Elsie's' right side (the proper side). I pushed the top of my head against her flank and when the man said "GO!" I began stripping.

Beautiful, fragrant, fresh warm milk began to flow. Mmmm.

One minute later Nabors had a few dribbled drops of milk. I had a large glassful.

Game over. Paul wins.

Paul and 'Elsie'.

Heh, Heh, Heh!

No Fair!!!

I grew up around Holstein cattle – we had them on our farm. I learned how to hand-milk a cow when I was ten!

The only way this could have been better is if I'd still been Em- peror Rodgers, milking in my royal purple tunic!

During that era radio was fun. We did stuff like this all the time.

Just like "WKRP in Cincinnati."

Ron Nabors and Paul Rodgers at the Fair.

The Baltimore Colts

WCBM was the flagship station for the Baltimore Colts Radio Network, with longtime Baltimore broadcaster Fred Neil at the helm as producer. Players were frequent visitors to the station – the stuff of legend for any football fan.

(These were the genuine NFL Colts, not the present day interlopers. And no! I'll never give in!)

SIDEBAR: I became a Colts fan in 1956, shortly after they were born. I was dating Barbie, and we watched in her Dad's game room when the Colts won 'The Greatest Game Ever Played', defeating the New York Giants in the first overtime game in NFL history. Many legends were born on that day.

Imagine my excitement when, in 1965, I scored four season tickets on the thirty-five yard line, about thirty rows up from the field behind the Colts bench.

I say 'my' excitement, but I gotta tell you, Barbie loves football so it's really 'we'. (My Barbie is the perfect companion in many ways, one of which is – she understands football.)

We didn't have a lot of money, so those seven Sundays in the fall were a special treat for us.

We'd get a baby sitter and go to the game, then on the way home we'd stop for Chinese. Barbie took the sitter home while I set the table and got the food ready.

Then we'd sit down for dinner with our three children.

The 'rabidity' (rabidness?) of Baltimore Colts fans resulted in Memorial Stadium being dubbed 'The World's Largest Outdoor Insane Asylum'. It was well named.

The Colts played in the NFL West which provided us a rotation of Bears, 49'ers, Lions, Rams, Vikings, and of course the hated Green Bay Packers. The list of names that we applauded/booed every week is a roster of Hall of Famers.

We watched John Unitas, Raymond Berry, and Penn State's Lenny Moore compose and conduct the 'Two-Minute Drill' Symphony.

Saw Paul Hornung miss five field goals one afternoon.

Cheered as Gino, Artie, Lyles, and Bubba dominated on defense.

Pumped fists when #32 cold-cocked an unwelcome visitor, then recovered the football and handed it to the ref.

Stood in shocked silence when some bozo 'landed' a light plane in the upper deck.

Fast times on 33rd Street, indeed.

Artie, Syzzy & Brace

During football season the Szymanski-Donovan Show aired Friday evenings at 6 PM, following my show. Cohosts were former Colts center/linebacker (then General Manager) Dick Szymanski - #52, and Hall of Fame defensive tackle and raconteur Art Donovan - #70. Both men won multiple NFL championships – both were All-Pro on several occasions.

(By all that's righteous, Szymanski should be in the NFL Hall of Fame.)

In 1971, Szymanski turned over his spot 'on mic' to another NFL champion and All-Pro Colts player, defensive end Ordell Braase - #81. Braase owned a nice restaurant in Timonium which we frequented frequently. (Ummm, 'frequently frequented'? :-)

Szymanski-Donovan or Braase-Donovan … take your pick.

Artie called 'em 'Syzzie' and 'Brace' – they were the 'straight men' on an otherwise free-form radio program.

Discussion usually started with details of a previous game or an upcoming opponent.

Shortly after that, Donovan would volunteer a story and away they would go.

Simply Great Radio.

One evening somebody asked Artie about his weight. He said, "You know you're big when you sit in the bathtub and the water in the toilet rises."

Donovan's weight usually hovered around 290.

Here's another: "I was never overweight as a player. There was a clause in my contract that said I had to weigh in at 270 every Friday morning. I always made it. I'd have dinner on Monday, and then I wouldn't eat until Friday."

Chuck Thompson, a very deserving broadcast member of the Baseball Hall of Fame, did the play-by-play. Color was provided by Charley Eckman.

Thompson's smooth, flawless delivery painted vivid verbal pictures of the action. Eckman's growly color commentary left no doubt in the minds of the listeners: "This is football! For Men Only."

Closing Notes – The Class of WCBM

Charley Eckman passed away July 3, 1995, at age 74. Chuck Thompson died March 6, 2005, at age 83. Joe Knight passed away on Nov. 8, 2014 at 87. All are Baltimore legends.

In 1975, Richard Sher joined WJZ-TV where, in 1978, he and Oprah Winfrey cohosted "People Are Talking." Great chemistry there. This was Oprah's first gig as a talk show host.

Robert Burns went on to become a reporter for the Mutual News Network and for the Voice Of America.

John Hartge – (more about John later) also worked for Mutual, and closed out a distinguished career with many years as a reporter at the CBS Radio Network's Washington, DC Bureau.

Bob Schmidt was a featured reporter on the ABC Radio News Network for nearly three decades.

For over twenty years, Pat Nason worked in the Los Angeles office of United Press International, first as a UPI Radio Network reporter, and later (on the print side) as Entertainment Editor and a Desk Editor. At this writing, Pat is enjoying 'retirement', writing songs and performing with this band, Pat Nason and The Regular Crew. Check 'em out on YouTube. They make great music.

In addition to producing the radio play-by-play for the Colts, and coercing Howard Cosell into defaming me, Dave Humphrey served as Morning News Anchor at WCBM thru 1985, then as News Director at WLIF. In 1993 he became Director of External Affairs in the State of Maryland's Dept. of General Services. During that period he worked for four Maryland Governors, retiring in 2011.

In the Golden Era of Baltimore radio, WCBM was one of the great stations. I was blessed to be a small part of it.

But this phase of my career was about to end.

CHAPTER THIRTEEN

GOIN' WITH THE FLO

In mid-1965 I was hired as a freelancer to be the Baltimore/Washington radio/TV voice for Montgomery Ward Department Stores, and later for Union Trust Bank of Baltimore. The Waltjen Agency handled these accounts. Account Manager, Bill Hevel, produced the commercials that we recorded several times each month.

Montgomery Ward wanted an uptempo 'pitch' style (an 8 out of 10 on my 'loud/obnoxious' scale).

Union Trust preferred the more 'banky' sound. Friendly. Factual.

You know … Businesslike.

As I recall, AFTRA scale required payment of $32.50 per radio commercial, $47.50 per TV voice-over, and $10 per hour for rehearsal time. If more than three commercials were recorded at any one session, we were paid for a second hour of rehearsal time, even if all was completed in one hour.

(These fees were increased every three years with the signing of each new union contract.)

A one-hour session that included the recording of one radio spot and one TV spot would yield $90.00. By comparison, my weekly salary at WCAO at this time was $250.00, so two sessions per month would easily provide me with gross income nearly equal to a week's salary.

This was fun and the income helped us to take good care of ourselves and our children.

I really wanted more freelancing.

Golnick, The World's Biggest

Baltimore's Leon Shaffer Golnick Agency was believed to be the world's largest producer of radio commercials, concentrating primarily on developing and syndicating campaigns for banks and auto dealers.

Their concept was simple ... and elegant.

A catchy slogan started the process, after which the Imagineers at the Golnick Agency would create a complete ad campaign: a radio jingle, ten to thirty radio spec spots both single and multi-voice, TV spec spots, print logos and layouts, etc. In other words, the whole megillah.

From the rich (and highly competitive) Baltimore-Washington talent pool, Golnick would select three to five voices to record the scripts. These 'spec spots' became an integral part of the master presentation.

One voice, the 'lead', was heard on all radio and TV spots.

When the campaign was assembled, it was given to Golnick's sales people who travelled North America presenting the campaign to potential clients. On a per-market basis, the first bank or auto dealer to lease the rights to the campaign owned its exclusive use in their market, for as long as they chose to pay Golnick the annual lease fee.

———

Golnick was one of the early syndicators of complete advertising packages. To small and medium market businesses across the US, the Golnick Agency offered major-market ad campaigns with quality and creativity that was otherwise unavailable in their markets.

This outstanding business model was a richly deserved smash hit for the Agency.

Every performer in the region wanted to work for the Golnick Agency.

Imagine being a voice in a Golnick campaign that was sold in twenty or more North American markets, a not-so-unusual occurrence. 'The Little Profit Dealer' is an example of one of those campaigns. The TV spots featured a bobble head doll dressed like Mahatma Gandhi. He was "The Little Prophet" – get it?

In creating the master campaign, suppose you were one of the voices on six of the fifteen radio scripts and two TV spots, and it took four hours to lay down the original campaign. You'd be paid $40 for rehearsal time, $195 for the radio spots, and $90 for TV – a total of $335 for the original session.

Suppose you were chosen to be the Lead Voice?

When a sale was made, the client got to choose which radio spots they wanted to use. When they chose spots that you were on you'd be called into the studio to rerecord that spot. Much of the time you'd only 'insert' the name of the new client into the 'boiler plate' – same script, just a different business name, but that didn't matter. To AFTRA, this was a new spot and required that the talent be paid for its recording.

Suppose you were the 'lead' voice and the campaign was sold in twenty markets or more?

What if you were on two or three different Golnick campaigns?

Golnick had its choice of talent and they selected only the best. Walt Teas, Flo Ayres, Joe Knight, Ed Walker, Larry Luman.

This 'work' was pure profitable fun.

The prestige was tremendous. The money was amazing.

I wanted in.

Really wanted in.

Audition
In April, 1970, Golnick called an audition. I signed up and eagerly awaited the opportunity to show my 'wares'.

Alas, the day of the audition I awakened with chills and fever. I was under the weather big time but there was no way I was going to miss this audition.

I sat nervously in the reception room.

It felt like a foreign country.

———

A voice on the intercom said, "Talent please."

I was taken to the studio and seated at a table in front a microphone.

A moment later, in walked the person with whom I would be performing.

None other than Walt Teas, legendary freelance voice of the region – the very best of the very best.

I felt like I'd just arrived in Timidated. You know? That foreign country where the unprepared go to perish?

I was cooked.

The worst was yet to come.

We got our scripts. The engineer gave us our cues.

Walt had the opening line.

Even before he finished I knew I was toast.

Teas was his magnificent self – the consummate radio actor.

I was just another announcer with a 'big voice'.

Walt acted his first line. I read mine.

In a millisecond it was crystal clear to me.

I simply had no idea what I was doing. And I had no business whatsoever to be participating in this audition.

After one script the producer said, "Thank You." I left for home.

This was to be the most embarrassing moment of my career.

I'd done many auditions, some successful, some not. But this was the first I'd ever done while being totally unprepared.

While very real, the chills and fever had nothing whatsoever to do with the result.

I had no excuse. I was simply not ready for the freelance Big Leagues.

Worse, I was clueless about what I could do to affect a different result.

I was good on the air. People said I had a great voice. I believed I did a nice job on recorded commercials.

Whatthehelljusthappened?

Color me humbled.

Not Rhode Island

Late that summer, providence appeared. The Baltimore Sun published an article about a course in radio acting to be offered by Goucher College and taught by a nationally-recognized freelance performer.

The teacher?

'Twas to be none other than 'The Lady of a Thousand Voices,' the inimitable Ms. Flo Ayres.

The article stated that the course was primarily for Goucher College students, but went on to say that a few spots might be open to the public.

I had never met Flo but I felt as if I knew her. Her distinctive voice and style graced many of the best ad campaigns in the region. She was 'top-drawer' talent, every bit as good as June Foray, the voice of Rocket J Squirrel among others.

If memory serves, I believe the tuition was $300.

––––––

Next day I told one of the guys at WCBM what I was about to do.

"What? You're gonna make a fool of yourself. You're gonna attend a class with a bunch of college girls, trying to learn what you already know how to do? Ridiculous! You're a professional – one of Baltimore's top radio personalities. Your voice work sounds great. It's crazy. I'd never do something like that."

Easy for him to say. He never read with Walt Teas.

I enrolled immediately.

School's In Session

Our 'classroom' was Flite 3 Studios, located just fifteen minutes from the radio station.

We were to meet for three hours each Wednesday evening, for thirteen consecutive weeks. Class would be called to order promptly at 6:30.

The student body consisted of eight or ten Goucher girls, Elane Stein (surprise of surprises), and yours truly, Paul Rodgers.

Baltimore's #1 Audio Engineer, Louis Mills, was on the console.

It took Flo less than three minutes to get started.

Proper introductions, three minutes of straight talk, and away we went.

Ms. Ayres removed a handful of scripts from her briefcase and handed me one.

"Paul, please record this 30-second script for us. Go on Louis' cue."

It was a spot for Valley View Farms, a Cockeysville, MD nursery advertising, "… a large selection of beautiful flowering plants and bushes just in time for spring planting …" and telling folks why they should shop at Valley View.

I went over the script, the music started, Louis threw me a cue, and I read.

Flo asked for the playback. Louis obliged. The class listened attentively.

(Mmm, not too bad, sez I)

Playback over. Five seconds of silence.

Flo broke … no, she fractured the silence.

"Paul, you could read the Declaration of Independence, the soliloquy from Hamlet, and this Valley View spot, and they'd all sound exactly the same."

I felt as if I'd had the wind knocked out of me.

Howard Cosell imitation: "Mr. Paul Rodgers. Top radio personality. Hotshot DJ. Dropped like a bad habit. Crushed like a prom corsage. Reduced to a shadow of his former self. Stripped of all illusion and dignity."

Flo took the script from my hand. "What? No script mark-up?"

(Huh? Whatthehell is 'script mark-up'?)

I had no clue what she was talking about.

"How can you expect to interpret this script … present the proper feeling from the words … the flow of the thought … without first reading through the script and marking up accent points? Here, let me show you."

In forty seconds Flo 'marked up' the script. Then she recorded her version.

Wow!

Flo's reading sounded like spring … honey bees … warm May breezes. I could smell roses and lilacs. I wanted to jump in my car and go to Valley View Farms. I wanted to put on jeans and start planting flowers.

Mine? Yecch.

Sounded like I was in a hurry. Nice voice, but … .

Louis played the spot again. I listened intently, my mind's eye recalling Flo's body movements as she read.

Flo wasn't 'reading' a script … she was reciting a story.

She moved closer to, then away from, the microphone, using it as a 'tool for expression' (which she later demonstrated).

Her hands and arms moved instinctively and expressively as she told the tale.

Her facial expressions and the tone and timbre of her voice changed appropriately as she accented the meaning of each word and phrase.

Flo was playing the part of a woman who was simply overjoyed with the prospect of sharing her wonderful secret known as Valley View Farms.

This was far more than 'recording spots'. This was a performance.

Flo was creating theatre in the mind of the listener.

Radio 'acting' at its finest.

And I got it.

In listening to the replay I heard what I'd lacked at that April audition, and I made a vow to use my time with Flo to learn how I might someday be able to emulate such a performance.

I was confident that by the end of the course, with more lessons and lots of practice, practice, practice … I'd be ready.

About Flo
By the time I met Flo, she'd already recorded thousands of commercials and syndicated programs.

She'd done narration for National Geographic, Sea World and AARP, and hosted many radio shows. And she'd taught radio and communications at John Hopkins University, Goucher College, and Towson State University.

(Wow. A measly $300 has put me in the presence of the mind and talent of this wonderful and accomplished lady. Flo Ayres is going to be my teacher.)

What a privilege.

For the next thirteen Wednesdays we marked up scripts, recorded spec spots – single and multiple voice – did lots of 'in character' improv (Flo selected the topic. Elane was a star).

Flo taught us phrasing and proper script mark-up. She showed us how to 'bring the microphone to life'.

"Put yourself in the role," she used to say.

She generously shared her extensive knowledge and experience with all of us.

———

Graduation Day was history's shortest graduation ceremony.

We followed up our last class with an in-studio party. We thanked Flo for putting up with us. She allowed as how she enjoyed it.

She called me aside and said, "Paul, you're ready. You're gonna do fine."

I felt like a million.

In retrospect, Flo's original critique of my first read was spot on. I needed to hear serious, honest criticism from a person who knew what she was talking about. She hit me right between the eyes.

Just what I needed.

Cattle Call
About three months later the Golnick Agency asked for auditions. Thirty people showed up. They planned to hire three voices – two male, one female.

I was one of the males.

Without guidance and instruction from Flo Ayres, this would forever have been an elusive dream. I owe Flo Ayres, big time.

———

Today, Feb. 18, 2014. I googled 'Flo Ayres' and got her contact information.

I called and spoke with Flo for twenty minutes. It was a wonderful conversation.

Flo is doing well in retirement, but my bet is she really hasn't retired … not completely. She should never retire.

She's a high energy lady with great talent, both of which need an outlet. Besides, people are waiting to hear more of her work.

———

Fifty-three seconds is all you'll need to 'get' what Flo Ayres brings to the communications industry…and what she taught (and brought) to me.

To hear the audio definition of the word 'talent' please go online to voice123.com/floayres. The menu in the right sidebar provides access to her audio files. Enjoy.

Flo Ayres at voice123.com
https://voice123.com/profiles/floayres/

As a teacher, Flo reminded me of Mrs. Rose Harer, my high school English teacher, a mentor who almost singlehandedly got me into college.

Potential hurt feelings be damned, Mrs. Harer never feared telling her students the honest truth. To pass her English course a student had to give their very best every day. Mrs. Harer always knew. That is also Flo.

CHAPTER FOURTEEN

EXIT AT THE TOP

It was 1972. Much had changed.

WCBM had a new General Manager whose opening gambit set a new tone at the station. Can you say 'morose'?

On his first day in office, the new GM called a staff meeting that remains in my mind as Chapter One, Verse One from the corporate management handbook titled "How To Demoralize A Staff In One Sentence."

WCBM was kicking some serious fanny. Ratings were excellent and business was exceptional. In one part of the building a small (but perceptible) change of attitude had occurred (more on that in a minute), but otherwise we were smokin'.

As if to intentionally undermine the Aura of Excellence that permeated the building, our new GM opened his first staff meeting with this:

"Morale is down around here."

Oh yes ... he said that. Really – he did.

He was right. Morale had dropped. It dropped in the very moment those words came out of his mouth.

Hit the floor with a thud.

This was my first major experience with that pesky 'self-fulfilling prophecy' thing.

Union Benefits

The WCBM news staff decided they needed to join AFTRA (American Federation of Television and Radio Artists).

Twenty-three on-air people were involved in the voting. Twelve voted yes, eleven voted no, and WCBM became an AFTRA station. I was a 'no'.

I can't speak to what the 'yes' voters had in mind but here's what I 'gained'.

I had to give up the one weekend off per month that I'd negotiated in my contract.

I'd been working six-day weeks for fifteen years. This was never a burden but it was a pain, because the obligation to be in-studio on that sixth day made it impossible to plan very much of a normal weekend.

My three children were involved in sports and school activities, so I chose Sunday as my sixth day. Having one two-day weekend each month was like owning gold.

No more.

Next, I had to give up one of the four weeks of vacation that I'd also negotiated. The AFTRA contract provided for three weeks of vacation after three years employment.

Worst of all, I was no longer eligible to participate in the Metromedia Profit Sharing Plan. Company policy stated that this was only available to non-union employees.

Participation in the profit sharing plan was as follows: After one year of employment, non-union employees could contribute up to ten percent of salary in excess of the Social Security maximum, which the company matched each year. (At that time the SS maximum was $6,500.)

I was earning $20,800. After subtracting $6,500, I could contribute $1,430 per year, which the company matched every year.

For 1970, '71 and half of '72 I'd contributed a total of $7,150 into my account, which was closed on the day the station went union. A week or so later I received a closeout check for more than $15,000, an astronomical return on investment.

Oh well.

Change Gotta Come
I loved WCBM. Takin' Baltimore home from work was a blast.

Our audience was 'interactive' before that became a common concept.

We asked 'em to do stuff ... and they did it. When there was an on-location broadcast they turned out, sometimes en masse.

We loved 'em up. They returned the love.

After ten years on the air in Baltimore, my name was fairly well recognized and I was getting to participate in some pretty neat stuff.

But by early summer of 1972 things just weren't the same. Staff attitudes seemed to be flagging.

I began to tire of the proceedings.

———

The summer of 1972 was hot and humid, typical of Baltimore, but one early August evening had produced a loud thunderstorm followed by a cool front – a rare occurrence for August in Baltimore County.

Next morning around seven, our bathroom curtains moved gently to the rhythm of a cool breeze as I stood in front of the mirror, shaving. I was totally lost in thought.

(I don't get it. For absolutely no reason I've been tired lately, and I sure haven't been doing a very good job. Goin' through the motions ... doin' my show every day ... some days good, some days not so good ... either way is OK. No one seems to notice. This isn't me. Something is very wrong.)

And it hit me.

Before WCBM, every day I'd been striving to improve and learn more about radio. And whenever I believed I'd learned all I could learn from my current place of employment, I moved on. And thankfully, always up.

At WCBM I'd reached the point where I'd learned all they could teach me.

For a couple years I'd been earning great money doin' what I do. It was fun. But it was easy for me. Too easy.

I'd gotten lackadaisical, lost focus, stopped striving.

And with no new challenge to conquer, I'd stopped giving.

In that cool morning, standing in front of the mirror, I saw the truth … and instantly I knew this was something that needed to be addressed.

Exactly how I wasn't sure.

The answer was just a few hours away.

SIDEBAR: In her book, *Light on the Path* (first published in 1885), Mabel Collins wrote, "For when the disciple is ready the Master is ready also."

Some forty years later this had morphed to "When the student is ready the teacher will appear," and was attributed to Buddha. But Mable said it. Mable Collins.

Just setting the record straight.

Just Around The Corner

At two that afternoon I was back on the air, 'doin' the do'. 'Round three-fifteen the studio phone lit up.

It was my friend and radio 'partner', Kerby Confer.

We hadn't worked together for three years. Kerb had left on-air radio to host a teen dance show on TV – the Dick Clark of Baltimore. And he'd taken the next step toward his (our?) sworn goal of owning a radio station – he'd been named Manager of WYRE, a small station in Annapolis, MD near where he lived, some 70 miles from my Hampstead, MD home.

We'd stayed in touch, but kid's schedules and the six-day work week made it difficult to get together.

We hadn't seen one another in over a year.

We said our hellos and chatted for a minute. Then: "So ... whatever happened to the guy who wanted to own a radio station?"

"Hey, he's still here. You're talkin' to him."

"Well, are you making any headway toward that goal?"

"Ahh ... mmm ..."

"Looks to me like you're doin' the same stuff you've been doing for the last ten years."

"Yeahhhh ..."

"Right. So no progress, right?"

"Well, I wouldn't say that ..."

"Hey. You're caught in the Velvet Whipsaw. We need to talk. Grab Barbie and the kids and come down for the Labor Day weekend. You can stay with us ... we'll take the station's boat for a ride on the Chesapeake Bay, and we'll talk ... like old times."

I took Sunday and Labor Day as vacation days and we went to Annapolis.

————

Two families together, four adults and six kids. A group of friends cruisin' the Chesapeake Bay aboard the station's boat, Voice Of The Bay.

Kerb's piloting the boat and we're talking.

"Here's the deal. To be a successful owner you'd need to learn the business end of the business, right? It begins with sales because that's where we get the money to run the business.

"I want you to come to work with me at WYRE … doing the morning show and selling the rest of the day. Marvin Mirvis owns the station and he'll show you the ropes. He's a great businessman and a terrific person. You'll love Marvin.

"I can only pay you half what you're earning now, but the timing is perfect. If this works out we'll have our own station in three to five years … maybe sooner."

(Whoa … fifty percent pay cut … sixty-seven mile drive to the station … the morning show, meaning a three:thirty wake-up call … Top 40 format. But … first step on the road to ownership. Much to consider.)

"I assume it's a five-day week, right?"

"Yep."

"And I can continue with my freelance sessions?"

"If you can schedule 'em in the afternoon, yes. And by the way, if you can write $100,000 in ad sales the first year, and if you show leadership qualities, you'll be named Sales Manager next March and be off the air."

"I'm in."

Well, it wasn't quite that way, but almost.

Barbie was in on the conversation. She'd always supported whatever I wanted to do with my career. We talked later that evening and I showed her we'd be OK financially.

Barbie said, "Go for it."

The actual "I'm in" came the following day.

We drove home Monday afternoon and I called my Mom that evening to let her know what I was planning.

I gave her chapter and verse, and she asked, "Are you confident that this is the right thing, not just for you but for your family?"

"Mom, there's not a doubt in my mind."

"Follow your heart."

(This was to be the last conversation I had with my dear mother. She fell gravely ill a few days later and slipped into a coma. She passed away on October 24, 1972.)

Tuesday, September 5, 1972, I resigned my position at WCBM.

———

Program Director, Dale Andrews, asked when I needed to leave. I said two weeks.

"Paul, our summer ratings were the best ever and the fall rating period starts Thursday. Can you stay through the rating period?"

"That won't end until Thanksgiving."

"Right, but your summer numbers are the best in the entire book – the highest ratings in the city. I need time for a transition to whoever's going to replace you. First quarter would be best for that."

"I'll ask."

Kerb said, "No hurry. If that's what you feel obligated to do, it's OK. December will be fine."

———

Note: I was aware that our ratings were good, but had no idea that PM Drive on WCBM were 'best'. Rarely are the ratings for one personality reflective of the work of just that one person. He/she may be important, but far more often the ratings reflect the totality of the station's content. I believe that was the case here. WCBM was a great radio station.

Full Disclosure: In a sort of egotistical way, I saw my choice as similar to that of Jim Brown who retired from pro football at the peak of his success. I was leaving at the very top of my game because 'it was time' and because there were other things I wanted/needed to accomplish.

The GM
Our by now infamous morale-boosting GM was told that I'd accepted a position at a 250 watt daytime only radio station in a small market, and that in addition to learning sales I'd also do mornings because the company couldn't afford to pay me 'straight up' – they were forced to 'dollar-average' me to justify hiring me to sell media, and that I'd chosen this path because I wanted to own a radio station.

"What? He's a disc jockey. Disc jockeys can't sell advertising. And they certainly aren't businessmen. He's gonna fall flat on his face. Guaranteed.

"And own a station? Puhlleeze. That'll never happen either. He'll be knockin' down our door in six months."

My last show on WCBM was Saturday, December 2, 1972.

Monday, Dec 4, I was the morning guy on WYRE ... and a media salesperson.

WYRE'd

WYRE was a local Annapolis radio station – a 250 watt daytime only station located between Baltimore and Washington, DC, and under the shadow of thirty or forty highly-rated, large footprint metropolitan radio signals. One would think there's no way WYRE can succeed.

One would be incorrect.

AM radio station coverage is enlarged when a station's tower and ground system sit on/in wet ground, the wetness acting like a radiator – a serious 'booster' of the station's broadcast signal. The WYRE tower was on a sort of swampy piece of ground located next to the Spa Creek. The radials were laid out in that field. The Spa Creek feeds directly into the Chesapeake Bay.

On dry land, the prime signal coverage of a 250 watt AM station is a radius of twelve miles which, going west and northwest, was the case with WYRE. However, going north and south along the west shore of the Bay, and on across the water, WYRE could be heard from Havre de Grace, MD to Occoquan, VA, fifty miles in each direction.

Realizing this, WYRE station ownership decided to provide specific programming that no metropolitan station could (or would) ever match. Sitting at 810 on the AM dial, the station became "Boat Radio Eight, WYRE – The Voice of the Bay."

The music format was Top 40, similar to Baltimore's WCAO. But WYRE's information package set the station apart from every station within a hundred miles.

The top and bottom of every hour featured WYRE Marine Accu-Weather Forecasts for the Chesapeake Bay, delivered by Cadets from the Annapolis Coast Guard Station (can you say 'authentic').

WYRE Marine Weather
http://emperorrodgers.com/WYRE_weather.mp3

Tide timetables, fishing reports, sailing club meetings, fishing derbies, basically any boating related events were regular features of WYRE programming.

Local and regional boat dealers and other large marine-oriented businesses were present at the boat shows in New York, Baltimore, Washington and Annapolis, so WYRE broadcast 'live' from those shows each year.

From April through October, the weekend population floating on the Bay in boats was equal to that of Frederick, MD, the state's second largest city.

True, WYRE had many local listeners, and plenty more of the traditional radio advertising clients. But it was the 'bonus market' provided by the massive local/regional boating industry that made the business hum. Example: WYRE's Marine Weather Forecast Sponsorships were sold out April thru October – with a waiting list.

Most of the WYRE air staff were folks who'd worked as part-timers on top Baltimore/Washington stations, but hadn't yet been able to break into full time. Dennis Constantine was the PD. Jim Tice, Ed Gursky, Paul Cavanaugh, Howard Dicus, Charlie Lake, Chris Saunders … these and so many other young people would learn and grow at WYRE, then go on to have outstanding careers in radio.

Sales Manager
I was fortunate to have great success in radio sales, primarily due to the wonderful training and encouragement I received from WYRE's owner, Marvin Mirvis.

By February of 1974 I'd reached my goal of $100,000.00 in radio sales. Marvin had purchased a radio station in New Jersey and was transferring WYRE's Sales Manager to that station.

I was named Sales Manager of WYRE.

Music
For seventeen years it was a privilege for me to be on the radio, "… playing records and saying funny stuff." It's impossible to measure the love I had (and have) for much of the music I got to present to our listeners.

In my Top 40 days I favored rhythm and blues artists like James Brown, Chuck Willis, Joe Tex, Etta James, and Ivory Joe Hunter.

Otis Redding stood tall – much taller than any other. No one ever 'begged' like Otis.

And Dinah Washington. And the astonishingly wonderful Patti LaBelle.

Chuck Berry stood and played guitar. Fats Domino sat and played piano.

And I loved the Sun Records stars – early Elvis, Carl Perkins, Gene Vincent and the Blue Caps, Jerry Lee Lewis and Johnny Cash.

Doo-Wop groups like the Dubs (Could This Be Magic), the Five Satins ([Closer] To The Aisle), Lee Andrews and the Hearts, the Five Keys, The Jive Five and so many, many more.

Buddy Holly and the Crickets were fabulous. Roy Orbison made 'em cry. Frankie Valli and the Four Seasons – wow. The Tams were a fave of mine, especially Untie Me.

Motown gave us Marvin Gaye, the Miracles, Mary Wells, the Supremes, and the greatest show group of all time, the tempting Temptations. (I always wanted to sing bass and do a set with the Temps).

Bob Dylan. The Beatles. All you need to do is say the names. In their own genres they compiled the greatest of all songbooks, post-1955.

Elton John, Billy Joel, Paul Simon and Art Garfunkel. The Eagles (Americas greatest group), the Chi-Lites, David Gates and Bread. Karen Carpenter, Dionne Warwick, Dusty Springfield.

Impossible to list them all.

During my seventeen years on the air, it often seemed to me as though I was one of the session musicians or a singer on the 'biscuits' I was spinning.

And by the way – the studio speakers were turned up loud. Really loud.

Grab some of these goodies and give 'em a listen.

I Don't Wanna

In 1958, Chuck Willis recorded a song called (I Don't Wanna) Hang Up My Rock 'N' Roll Shoes. It was the 'A' side of what would soon become a two-sided hit. (The 'B' side was "What Am I Livin' For [If Not For You].)

I first heard 'Rock 'N' Roll Shoes' a few months after I got my first job in radio. Can you say, 'Love at first listen'?

During the summer of 1958 I played the record many times, and by that fall I'd made a decision – when the day comes that my on-air career as a Disc Jockey is over, this is the record that'll be playing as I walk out the studio door.

That date was Friday, March 1, 1974.

For the first time in forever I didn't sign off with the goodbye I'd used for more than ten years: "Keep the garbage can covered, the dog tied tightly, and the baby fed. And until we meet again, Yats Esool."

On this day Chuck Willis' "(I Don't Wanna) Hang Up My Rock and Roll Shoes" played as I walked out the studio door.

The following Monday we took the family to Disney World.

Paul Rodgers Hangs Up His Rock 'N' Roll Shoes (2:55)
http://emperorrodgers.com/WYRE_HangsItUp.mp3

Paul Rodgers' final full hour on the air (56:44 min.)
http://emperorrodgers.com/WYRE_FinalHour-1974.mp3

———

By the mid-fifties, the ascendant popularity and sales of 'black' music among young Americans was forcing 'white' radio stations to play these records.

Through this period, Chuck Willis had many #1 Hits on the Billboard R&B Charts, and in 1957-'58 five of his songs made the Billboard Top 100 Pop Music Charts. What Am I Living For sold over one million copies and earned Willis a Gold Record, awarded posthumously.

In a cruel twist of fate, Hang Up My Rock 'N' Roll Shoes and What Am I Living For were to be the last two songs Chuck Willis would ever record. He died of peritonitis on April 10, 1958, just eighteen days before this record first appeared in the Billboard Magazine Top 100. A beautiful career cut short at age 30. Very sad.

The Rocket Ship

Many people viewed WYRE as a small station.

In many important ways, WYRE was a Rocket Ship. Marvin Mirvis was the pilot, and many of his crew went on to enjoy great careers in radio (see the Epilogue for details).

As for Kerby Confer and Paul Rothfuss – they were boyhood friends who made a pact, and then rode their bikes off a cliff into the social disruption that was Top 40 Radio.

With more guts than brains, but with a ton of hands-on real world experience and a briefcase full of lessons learned, they traded in their bikes for their own radio rocket ship and rode it into the future.

If you want to read about that rocket ride, or get notice of other cool books and fun stories from this writer and publisher, sign up for our newsletter at:

R | L Publishing, LLC
http://rlpublishers.com/

EPILOGUE

THE SEARCH FOR KING AUGUST 1

Whilst looking through old pictures to include in this book, I came across the King August I stuff I'd saved since late 1964 and early 1965.

I reread it and laughed like hell. Again.

I decided this was an absolute 'Must Include'.

I also thought it would be nice to give credit to its creator but I didn't know his name.

In looking over the material I noticed a very small faded return address on the back of one envelope. A clue to the identity of King August I?

The letter had been mailed from Linthicum, MD, a Baltimore suburb. Post date on the envelope was December 14, 1964.

Maybe a starting place – but wait.

It's 2017. Do folks live in the same house … for fifty-three years?

Kids grow up and leave home, right? Would the 'King' still live at this address? Or any member of his family? Would neighbors know who lived there in 1964? What are the chances?

Slim and none, I reckoned.

I reached out on Facebook.

Crickets.

Next, I contacted Mark Smith, a childhood friend of my oldest son. Mark has lived in the Baltimore area his entire life.

I explained what I was trying to accomplish and gave Mark the address. He said he'd take a look.

In a few days Mark sent me an email complete with a picture of the house. "Yep, the house is still there."

I asked if he'd mind going to the house to ask the resident if they knew who lived there in the early sixties.

The longest of long shots, right?

200-1 at best.

You won't believe this.

A day or two later Mark called to tell me that the current resident had been in the house for about twelve years and that he'd be happy to talk with me.

I called him and learned...

... wait for it ... wait for it ...

... he bought the house from its original owners, a family named Hartge. He told me they had a son named John and he thought they were in their late seventies when the house was sold.

This was the 'key' that eventually unlocked the puzzle.

––––––––

Hartge is an unusual and very distinct surname. When I heard it I began to think ...

What if?
At WCBM in 1971 and '72 I worked with a talented, probably 22-year-old news reporter named ... John Hartge.

I couldn't stop trying to put two and two together.

(Can it be? Nah. Impossible.)

If John Hartge had been King August I, surely he would have mentioned something to me when we worked together. Or at least mentioned the Emperor.

That's what radio people do, right? They talk? Nary a peep.

––––––––

I hadn't heard anything about John Hartge since the mid-'70s when he was on the air at the Mutual News Network.

Even if he was King August I ... how'm I gonna find him to ask?

And besides – Can this be? Really? What are the chances?

––––––––

Believing that one of the other ex-WCBM'ers might know of John's whereabouts, I contacted Pat Nason with whom I'd stayed in touch over the years.

I sent Pat an email explaining that I was doing some research on the people we'd worked with at WCBM (Pat was one) but I'd been unable to locate John Hartge.

"Pat, can you help me with this?"

"Oh, yeah. Maybe. Last time I heard, John was working for the CBS Radio Network at their Washington, DC bureau office. I have a pal who worked there. I'll get back to you."

(Bingo?)

Pat sent my email to his friend, who then put John and Pat in touch, the first contact they'd had in years.

Pat told John of my 'research project' and suggested that he contact me.

Next day I got an email from John, then a phone call.

Fess Up

John and I hadn't talked for forty-five years. As our conversation unfolded it seemed to me that little time had passed. (As I said earlier, radio keeps you young!)

We exchanged pleasantries … got caught up on some personal stuff, and for ten or fifteen minutes shared memories of WCBM and the great times we enjoyed at this outstanding radio station. It was really sort of a laugh fest.

Then … "Listen John, I don't want you to think I'm pulling a 'funny' on you and I never want to be surreptitious.

"It's true – I am doing research on the WCBM news staff and the great people I worked with there. You're part of that which is why I wanted us to talk.

"But I want you to know – I have another quite separate reason. An ulterior motive, if you will.

"I'm writing a book about Baltimore radio in the '60s. It'll include a chapter about Emperor Rodgers and the Royal Commandos and how our listeners responded to this whacky promotion.

"So I gotta ask: Are you King August I?"

From the initial noise John made I knew I'd caught him completely off guard.

(Awuhcchk-mwfff-cough) "Aww geez. (nhhgh) I can't believe this. Are you kidding me?

(string of laughter) "I wondered when this would come back to haunt me."

Can you believe this?

I couldn't stop laughing.

I soon learned that King August I was the creation of not one but two high school friends (still friends) from Linthicum, MD. Michael Vogelman, the cartoonist who became a high school teacher, and John Hartge, who had a very successful broadcast news career.

———

Really? After all these years?

So ... in 1964, two fifteen-year-old boys respond to a nutty radio promotion – The Emperor – by (anonymously) sending some really clever stuff about a fictional 'King August I' to the disc jockey.

Because the material was so creative and funny the DJ saved it in a scrapbook.

Six years later (1970) fate finds the DJ and one of the boys working together at a different radio station, the DJ playing records and saying funny stuff every afternoon from two to six, and the 'kid' (by now a college graduate and a true broadcast professional) covering and reporting the news.

The kid knew he was King August I and that years earlier he'd sent whacky stuff to the DJ.

The DJ didn't know.

The 'kid' never said a word.

Forty-seven years later the DJ decides to write a book and wants to include the King August I stuff. He has no clue re who (or where) the King might be. How to find King August I ... and to learn that 'he' was two guys!?

Now you know.

Impossible, right?

Note: August first is John Hartge's birthday.

It figures.

Michael Vogelman

Michael Vogelman is the 'other half' of King August I. He's the artist who, as a high school student, conceived and drew the crazy characters seen in Chapter 8A of this book.

When I contacted Michael (January 2018) I expected to find a fellow who'd spent large parts of his life as a graphic artist and who was still 'at it'. What I learned was that he was a high- chool teacher who had spent lots of spare time designing sets for class plays and other school activities. And in all this time he'd never been involved in cartooning or anything of the sort.

It took some cajoling but Michael agreed to contribute an original drawing to our book.

We are proud to present more evidence of the Genius of Michel Vogelman, circa 2018.

ON THE SHOULDERS OF OTHERS

My on-air career was successful for three important reasons.

One, I was raised to understand the importance of a high level work ethic. Two, I encountered many unselfish people who were in a position to provide me with guidance ... and who provided same. And three, I was fortunate to work with staffs of talented on-air people who would have served to make the radio stations successful whether or not I was there.

I want our readers to know something about how things turned out for them.

<u>Family</u>
Starting at an early age my father and mother instilled 'work ethic' in me.

From my Dad: "When you work for someone, treat his business as if you were the owner." And, "There's no such thing as 'that's not my job'. If you see something that needs to be done, do it." And from my Mom: "Treat everyone as if they're family. Kindness never fails." From both of them: "Always do the right thing and always behave like a gentleman."

Mom passed on Oct. 24, 1972; Dad on Aug. 13, 1975. The lessons I learned from them will be with me always.

There'll be more about my father (and other fine men) in our upcoming book, "DADS AND SUCH" and about my mother (and other fine women) in "MOMS AND SUCH."

Friends
My pal and partner, **Kerby Confer**, "Kerby Scott" on the air, was a very successful radio and TV personality in Baltimore/Washington.

In 1975 we achieved our 1958 goal of owning a radio station. This led to us forming Keymarket Communications, a company that from 1975 to 1987 owned/operated over fifty radio stations.

Kerby still owns radio stations and is an inductee of several Radio Halls of Fame.

Mentors & Role Models
Galen D. "Dave" Castlebury gave me my start in radio. By the late 1960s his stations were prosperous. Dave was elected a Lycoming County (PA) Commissioner and served several terms. He passed away in 2005 at age 75.

John Rosica was a record promotion man for RCA Records whose territory included Williamsport, PA. Not many of them came to this tiny market but John realized that this is where records got 'broken', that is, received airplay leading to sales, leading to recognition of 'hit potential' by stations in larger markets.

He came to our station and asked us to play his records. We were flattered so we played them. (Eventually, John became the National Promotion Director for RCA.)

John is one of the two men who told me about WSBA. He also made 'Famous Amos' famous, and turned doodling into an art form. Check this out:

The Art of Doodles
https://youtu.be/0vjpgNjGdwU

Then there was **Matty "Humdinger" Singer**, perhaps the most 'famous' promotion man on the east coast and a certified 'character'. He also told me about WSBA.

Matty knew the importance of visiting small market radio stations. He stopped by often, always with a stack of 'new hits' to promote. He asked us to play all of them. We mostly did.

When Matty passed, hundreds of people attended the celebration of his life. As with 'everything Matty,' this celebration was one of a kind.

Matty had recorded a message which he instructed his family to play at his celebration. The message went something like this: "As you will see I'm laid out on my stomach. That's so you all can come up and kiss my ass."

Matty was loved.

Al Saunders gave me all his wisdom and shared with me everything he knew.

Larry Monroe gave me a shot at the big time, a place to which I'd always aspired. He, too, became a radio station owner.

Frank Luber graciously wrote the Introduction to this book. He's been on radio and TV in Baltimore for almost sixty years.

As of this writing, Frank and Sean Casey are the morning team on WCBM, Baltimore's leading talk radio station. Frank sounds every bit as good as he always has. He's a Baltimore Radio legend.

Johnny Dark and **Jack Edwards** are also Baltimore Legends. Both were on the air there for more than fifty years.

Joe Kelly pirated me away from WCAO and gave me the opportunity to become a 'radio personality' on WCBM. The WCBM morning team of **Lee Case** and **Joe Knight** were great role models for me.

The invaluable lessons I learned from **Flo Ayres** continue to be of great help in my work as an audiobook narrator.

The Extended Radio Family

Many members of the WCBM News Staff went on to great careers.

Richard Sher teamed up with **Oprah Winfrey** on People Are Talking, the Baltimore TV show that launched her career. He also enjoyed a long and very successful career on WJZ-TV, both as a News Anchor and as creator and host of a number of Public Affairs programs.

Bob Schmidt was a featured news reporter for the ABC Radio Network. Both **Robert Burns and John Hartge** (aka 'King August I') worked for the Mutual Radio Network. In the 1990s Hartge joined the CBS Washington, DC News Bureau as part of its network news operation. He retired in 2011.

Dave Humphrey was News Director for WLIF-FM from 1985 to 1992. In 1993 he became Director of General Services for the State of Maryland where he worked for four Governors until his retirement in 2011.

Pat Nason worked in LA for United Press International and on the UPI Radio Network, eventually moving to print where he was appointed Entertainment Editor. He was a Desk Editor until his retirement in 2014.

Today Pat makes music in LA with 'The Regular Crew'. His "Good Old Fashioned American Boy" is terrific. Warning: Hear it once and you'll sing it all day! Pat's music is available for streaming or download at CD Baby, and on physical CDs directly from Pat. pnason@gmail.com

For Dennis Constantine, WYRE was the jumping-off place from which he launched a fabulous career as a major market Program Director at several top-rated stations. He's retired and living in Arizona.

After many years in broadcasting **Chris Saunders** became an Adjunct Instructor in the Governor's Office of Emergency Services in San Luis Obispo, CA, and was Director of News and Media Relations at the Thomas Jefferson School of Law in San Diego. Chris passed away in the summer of 2017.

Howard Dicus was the WYRE News Director. Today he's in Honolulu, Hawaii, hosting several popular and important radio programs there.

Jim Tice, Paul Cavanaugh, Ed Gursky, Charlie Lake, Madeline Waltjen, Sonny Ueberroth and so many other fine young people went on from WYRE to wonderful careers in broadcasting.

At one time or another we made a great team. Thank you one and all.

#

Contact The Emperor:
mailto:paul@emperorrodgers.com

Follow Paul "Emperor" Rodgers on Facebook:
https://www.facebook.com/phdwriter/

Read more from Paul "Rodgers" Rothfuss on his blog:
http://emperorrodgers.com/

Enlist in Rodger's Royal Commandos:
http://emperorrodgers.com/Commandos

Download a separate PDF file of the images and links contained in this book:
http://emperorrodgers.com/AER_images.pdf

#

93187273R00154

Made in the USA
Lexington, KY
13 July 2018